Childhood WITHDRAWN
UTSA LIBRARIES

DATE DUE

GAYLORD			... U.S.A.

D1018849

Antan d'enfance

Childhood

PATRICK CHAMOISEAU

Translated by Carol Volk

University of Nebraska Press : Lincoln

Publication of this translation was
assisted by a grant from the French
Ministry of Culture

⊖ The paper in this book meets
the minimum requirements of
American National Standard for
Information Sciences — Perma-
nence of Paper for Printed Library Materials, ANSI Z39.48-1992.

Library of Congress Cataloging-in-Publication Data
Chamoiseau, Patrick [Antan d'enfance. English] Childhood =
Antan d'enfance / Patrick Chamoiseau ; translated by Carol Volk.
p. cm. ISBN 0-8032-1487-1 (cl). – ISBN 0-8032-6382-1 (pa : alk. paper)
1. Chamoiseau, Patrick – Childhood and youth. 2. Authors,
Martinique – 20th century – Biography. I. Volk, Carol. II. Title.
PQ3949.2.C45Z46313 1999 843-dc21 (B) 98-27493 CIP

Contents

Translator's Note

I thought it would interest readers to see the letter that Chamoiseau sent to the translators of his novel *Texaco* around the world, which he was kind enough to send to me.

Dear translators,

Here are some of my writing principles:

1. In the use of French, I try not to forget my Creole language, my Creole imagination, my Creole conception of the world. This I would have done no matter what language I was using. It is therefore important that this Creole dimension of the text remain, in the words, the syntax, the images, and even in certain incomprehensible expressions. I do not sacrifice to transparency—no glossary, no footnotes, which, to my mind, contribute nothing from a literary/esthetic point of view. Not understanding everything with one's logic/reason/mind allows greater freedom in one's global perception, and thus turns out to be "richer" from a literary point of view, whether the interpretation is correct or false.

2. I use the entire French language. For me, there are no obsolete, out of date, unused, or vulgar words . . . I go from old French to contemporary slang. I travel the totality of the language, from its origins to today, everything is usable and everything is placed in the service of literary effect: old words, new words, scholarly words, technical words, slang words, hypercorrection and imprecise popular expressions . . . It's a language-fest! This I would have done in any language, and it would be best for this principle to remain.

3. I try to arrange it so that the language loses some of its pride and certainty, its formal academism. I want to feel it trembling, to feel its availability to all other languages of the world. I want it to stop behaving as if it were the only one capable of expressing

the world but rather for it to be relativised, informed of the splendid
possibilities of other languages, which are placed on the same plane.
I want the language to be "open."
   4. I sacrifice everything to the music of the phrase.

   Thank you and good luck!
                                                       Patrick Chamoiseau

I would like to thank Douglas Clayton for entrusting me with
this project, the MacDowell Colony and Yaddo for their support
during part of the work on the translation, and friends and
colleagues who gave me assistance and encouragement, in particular Sharon Guskin, Constance Herndon, Henry Hills, Henri
Israeli, Yuri Marder, Suzanne Seggerman, and Danny Vilmure.
Thanks to Cressida Leyshon of the *New Yorker*, Robert Winder
at *Granta,* Ingrid Muller, and the anonymous readers for the
University of Nebraska Press, who gave valuable input, as did
Chamoiseau himself.

Seek in oneself not — pretentiously —
the meaning of one's experiences, but
the place where they can be touched.

EDOUARD GLISSANT

> *O sharers*
> *You know how childhood is!*
> *(there's nothing left of it*
> *but we keep it all)*

Feeling

Can you tell of childhood what is no longer known? Can you not describe but survey it in its magical states, recover its mystery of clay and clouds, of stairway shadows and mad wind, and bear witness to the enclosure constructed while, plucking off petals of mystery and dream, you were taking inventory of the world?

Memory ho, this quest is for you.

And why this concealment, what is the meaning of these ruins, these empty landscapes, so wrongfully removed? Forgetfulness is on site, still clinging (powerlessly) and hunting the persistent emotion of fallen memories. What purpose does this plucker serve, leaving your high branches bare?

Childhood is a treasure whose geography you never clearly reveal. In it you mix up eras and ages, laughter and the illusion of having laughed, places and sensations that weren't even born there. You conduct an orgy of faces and sounds, of pain and lace, snippets of stories with no real origin, of ambiguous beings, loved or hated. They were important and still are, so much do you sketch them, carry them, preserve them — memory, why do you offer this treasure without ever really giving it?

And when from somewhere beyond the visible a batch of memories flows, unannounced and uncalled, when the illusory reckoning of a happy time rises in a burst of wind, when one reexamines this bewitching period in which every scrap of world gave a reading of the world's possibilities, in which the very reality of the world was a vague swarm of ants, all crazed, and when one feels there more exiled than foreign—is it I who remember, memory, or you who remember me?

Memory, let's make a pact long enough for a sketch, lower your palisades and pacify the savages, reveal the secret of the traces that lie at the edge of your brushy borders. I bring neither sack for kidnapping nor knife for conquest, nothing but intoxication and a mighty docile joy at the rhythm (flow of time) of your flow.

Let's make a pact.

Where does childhood begin? At the memory of one's first glimpse of the world? At the splatter of the visible-landscape against the earliest consciousness? The Prime Confidante speaks of an evening begun in pains. The suitcase was ready since after All Saints' Day. The journey took place on foot along the Levassor Canal, in the direction of the municipal hospital. At nine in the evening, a Thursday, yes, under the arc of December rains and winds, the midwife plucked the first cry, and the Confidante of today welcomed the last bit of her bowels. That was her Creole way of naming the fifth and—resolutely—the last of her children.

When, today, the latter expresses rather naive disbelief: But, Mama, why did you go there on foot? "Eti man té ké pwan lajan pou trapé loto-a?" "Where would I have gotten the money to pay for a car?" she replies, both proud and annoyed.

The man has had occasion to retrace this path of his birth. Down the Rue François-Arago, past the pungent cheer of the fish market, then alongside the canal to the Pont de Chaînes. He has also had occasion to taste Thursday evenings when nine o'clock finds Fort-de-France bathed in the yellowish points of the public light. He has had occasion, finally, to examine the

December evening storms when they erupted on Thursdays, with the desire to note not a sign, but a familiar sensation, a resurgence of the primordial impression. In vain. The man today has a melancholic weakness for rainy weather, damp winds, and nights turning to rivers. He might even have been a poet, perhaps, had these too blatantly beautiful preferences not been in such bad taste.

It was predictable in any case: the little black boy had nothing very special about him. Small, sickly, eyes without much light, consummating the art of whimsy, he set off catastrophes within himself at the slightest remark. He had a taste for being outside of the world, for remaining immobile on the roof of the kitch-ens, counting the clouds or transparently following the secre-tions of his pupils. During frenetic periods he climbed everything, like those marmosets whose corpulence, a little of the throat sound, and patience-trying energy he possessed. He was even (a vindictive older brother often affirms) a suckler until an age that defied reason. All day long, he is alleged to have vocalized this single cry on a cannibal beat: "Titac tété! Titac tété!" Without resorting to this lie, it would have been easy to predict the absence here of a true poet. His illusions alone deluded him into believing this babble during his adoles-cent crises.

His only genius was as a killer. He was anointed (by himself) king of the spiders and ants, of the dragonflies and earthworms, victims, nonetheless, of his massacres. He was the Attila of the red beetles and of the big dark cockroaches called *klaclac*. And he waged a campaign against a colony of rats that was impossible to destroy. This killer has a history—and here it is. It's doubtful he is proud of it.

It has its sources in periods of solitude inexplicable today, for the house was filled up. It was a large reef of wood from the north, stretching down the Rue François-Arago to the corner of the Rue Lamartine. At street level the Syrians, the owners of the building, had positioned their fabric stores. Right next to the entrance, opening onto the apartments' stairs, was a woodworking shop. The little boy never saw it but had always known of its existence: the carpenter, who went into sporting goods after a fire, had remained there, nostalgic for his bygone art. He conjured it up by useless repairs to every door and with ostentatious tools to warp the slightest nail. Behind his ear he kept an obstinate pencil. Standing on the doorstep of his store, his gaze lost in the crowd of madams seeking their customers, he used his pencil to take measurements of the world. No madam ever quite identified the object of this measurement. It was nonetheless precise: the fellow devoted time to it—arm extended, the point of his pencil emerging from between thumb and index, measuring the measure, measuring to measure, measuring, yes. . . . When the measurer died of a touch of congestion, no one thought to put the pencil in his grave. The little boy shed no tear; he alone knew the carpenter to be a wholesaler of sadness and measurer of an excess of ash.

The staircase led upstairs to where the families lived, the Ma Romulus family, the Ma Ninotte family, the Ma la Sirène family, the Ma Irénée family, the invisible family of an invisible junk dealer, partner of a near invisible customs officer in a sporadic, but passionate as possible, love. The traveling dealer was rarely there. She wandered the English isles and American coasts, from which she brought back illuminated fabrics, objects neither French nor Catholic, and perfumes capable of stirring spirits and hearts. Her presence in the apartment was as discreet as her absence, more discreet even than the colony of rats populating the labyrinths of the wooden stairs. It was signaled only by the rustling of merchandise unwrapped at night and repacked in small quantities intended for resale. This filled the minds of sleepers with a newspaper oratorio, the chinking of bottles, and the strange odor of genies in exile. But most of all her presence was signaled by the faithful customs officer, a little fat, a little sweaty, a little silent, very kind, whom the little boy of then thinks he saw laboriously climbing the steps of the stairs. In reality, thinking about it, he never saw him. He knew of him what was whispered nearly ten years later. Nor had he seen the traveling junk dealer (the apartment had been empty since before the little boy was even born), but his imagination could assign her an existence equal to the lingering aura of her distant passage. The other children were numerous, every family had four or five. They provided an explosive gang that raced down the hallway and stairs all the blessed day long. Which is why it is doubtful the little boy experienced periods of solitude, even if memories of his childhood begin, unfailingly, with moments of solitary immobility. This immobility would later instate him as an official observer of spiders, of ants, and of cockroaches—before, of course, turning him into a killer.

Under the staircase lay a zone of darkness favorable to shady lives. Piled there were demijohns, bottles, containers, packets of things that belonged to no one, or perhaps to forgetful families. From time to time, stacks of cardboard boxes signaled the arrival of Syrian products. Also found there were crates of every conceivable type, crates of cod, crates of red herring, crates of potatoes, which everyone concealed in expectation of a need. All this existed beneath a layer of dust, in an indescribable universe, until the day when Ma Ninotte (the little boy's mother) or Ma Romulus or Ma la Sirène, or else Ma Irénée, would be taken by a prophylactic rage and begin washing everything in a flood of water, showering it all with bleach and delivering heaps of refuse to the evening trash collectors. These sudden cleanings caused great upheaval. The little boy rediscovered a dead world beneath the tidying. Attentive and alone, he then watched as it progressively returned to its previous chaos, as life, with its receptacles and rubbish, brought it back to life.

Feeling 7

Spiders, ants, and cockroaches swarmed there. So much life in shadow enchanted the little boy. The spider webs unfurled in stiffened veils, shining, laden with the ashes of a dead moon. Broken by the daily recuperation of bottles, some twisted like ugly braids, while others unfolded into delicate embroidery, half effaced, shimmering in shadow, and revealing their cruelty by the subsequent disclosure of their trappings. Many cadavers hung there, dried-out trunks of pink gnats, of mosquitos, of tiny cockroaches, of *yen-yen,* of nocturnal butterflies caught in the snare of lace. It was all reminiscent of a celestial cemetery of tiny critters. The gravediggers were nowhere in sight and nothing seemed to be in charge. This enigma unraveled, boom, the day a fly happened to be ensnared before his eyes. The struggling insect shook the living, elastic geometry. Then the incredible happened. A long-fingered she-devil, finely attuned to the threads she seemed to be knitting, swiftly emerged from somewhere unseen, and pounced on her prey, fast as if gliding down a slide.

The fly saw himself covered and ceased—poof!—to fight. The spider wove him a whitish camisole fast-and-simple, then stopped still. The fly had become a cocoon adapted to an indefinable manner of eating, which the spider practiced with hearty appetite. Once the feast was over, she went to take up position in the nerve center of her web, connected to the vibratory language of her trap. The little boy subsequently saw her, and others still, and the entire troop, decimate little winged beasts. They were capable of enveloping several almost simultaneously. They scoured their tattered rags of web, the indiscernible limits of which were fanatically precise. He learned to attract them by shaking points on these webs. They hurried forth, found nothing, turned, and swerved back toward their headquarters. During the lookout, they made repairs, casting off from the end of shiny threads spun from the abdomen. Often, they caught themselves on broken fringes and tied them seamlessly, without a knot. The astonished little boy saw the ruin take on a perfect texture, and already he wondered how such genius could be at the service of so much cruelty. Fascinated by these evil culinary habits, he became king of the spiders by furnishing them with edibles. It was for them that he captured flies with the help of cups lined with sugar. For them that he imprisoned in jars a thousand tiny tribes of mosquitos captured on black cloths. For them that he lived with an eye riveted to the dust of the slatted shutters, to the joints of the corridor, to the dead angles of the stairs, tracking the tiny beast worthy of the arachnean holocaust. When habit dulled the interest of these executions, he stirred up fun by posing one spider on the web of another, or by supplying them with insects armed with carapaces, which they then had to tackle for some time before abandoning a part of their web. To do so, they patiently modified the lines of force, sending the trapped invader tumbling. Then he set about snipping the threads at points that destroyed the equilibrium out from under the panic-stricken creatures. Finally, before the age of fire, he began killing them.

He had discovered the miracle of matches and the power of the flame. The house was made of wood. Fires, along with floods and cyclones, made up the pantheon of Creole horrors. Ma Ninotte, who cooked in the apartment over a gas burner, performed a precautionary ceremony before lighting it. She began by silently moving the children aside. Slowly and majestically, she pumped the fuel, then, her eye sharpened, wielding a tiny needle, she unclogged the opening through which the flame would be fed. After a circular glance around, she proceeded to the lighting stage. And therein lay the mystery. For a split second the world was suspended on the edge of an intersection where everything was possible, especially disaster. Every living being prepared to make a run for it. Many were the cases of children singed bare, of shacks that disappeared in the gasp of flame, of lamps explosive as *chabines*. As a result, Ma Ninotte waxed philosophic about the power of fire, speaking sententiously in fifteen proverbs and three fine expressions. All this sufficed to inspire the little boy to steal a match, and then a box of them.

It was underneath the stairs that he explored the hazy reality of a flame: an orange impatience filled with transparencies and deep reds, arising from nothing, feeding on the wood of the match and suffocating on its own vitality. To contemplate a spark cast him into the antiquity of a preworld, into a pit of memory suddenly awakened to the most muffled fears. The little boy discovered anxieties within himself existing since time immemorial. He felt them flicker and grow silent to the sacred rhythm of the diminishing fire. Each match, aside from its mystery, brought him a rush of fulfillment, which he speedily sought in the next one. The box was gone in a snap, unless, before the last match, his dreamy stupor had permitted the fire to lick his finger. Then he dropped everything, horrified, his imagination torched, fleeing from the box as if from some hole into hell. Soon he returned, like the honeybee to her honey, and dipped into this dangerous happiness. But this age of fire was late in coming, in any case it followed that of massacres born directly from the discovery of the flame's power. It was later that he would learn that this force could be—for the tumults of childhood—a source of serenity.

The flame devastated everything. A miracle. The spider webs went up like straw. The spiders themselves were deified into shooting sparks. The little boy, master of the fire, made a clean sweep beneath the stairs. He was drunk with total destruction, drunk with savoring the enigma of a spider escaped from the cinders of its web. The spiders, although regularly set aflame, reproduced according to a law he liked to maintain on the level of a mystery (it was one of his rare virtues, this taste for pacts with incredible beings; he never lost it). Incited by a dearth of spiders, he brought fire to the cockroaches and ants. Columns of ants frequented syrupy remains on the bottles. Beneath the flame they lost their invisible pasture and were unable to converge for an et-cetera of minutes. Their hills went mad, oozed in every direction, and especially into the darkness of a newfound individuality. Nothing is more frenzied than ants ejected from their collective conditioning. Fire alone has this capacity to strike at their instinct and project them into themselves, onto themselves. As for the cockroaches, they either lost their wings in the crackling or rediscovered a frenetic usage of them. The child had to flee many times from beneath the stairs when his flame, having penetrated an inhabited chink in the wall, provoked first an emotional reaction from the larvae, then the flight of taciturn *klaclac* and of the venerable red roaches. They flew to attack his face, disgust him with their thorny legs, and inflict on him the indelible offence of their frightened musk. Who can say how many matches were consumed for the spiders to become rare, for the cockroaches to emigrate to the kitchens, and for the ants to bury themselves in oblivion. The little boy remained alone with his now useless weapon. He then set fire to corks, bottle labels, plastic, whose twisting he loved to observe. One day he lit a flame just for the sake of it, thus penetrating, yes, ever so gently, into the serenity of the magic age of fire.

The tool age was that of the Gillette blade. Papa was an elegant one. He shaved himself close and cultivated either a moustache or sideburns, depending on the fashion. He wielded foam and a screw-top razor, which had to be fitted with a daily blade. These blades, after their brief tour of duty, piled up useless. The little boy soon discovered their capacity to cut through anything. Since he couldn't very well shred the curtains, the mattress, or the books of his elders (who already found his existence trying, to say the least), the boy went off into his kingdom beneath the stairs, to cut off the legs of the surviving spiders and few remaining ants. He operated on the cockroaches (crucified with needles) for serious illnesses of which they were unaware but which justified a dissection in due and proper form. In addition to sicknesses, he sought hearts, lungs, blood, bones, a brain, a soul, ideas. He verified whether spiders and cockroaches could live without heads, or without stomachs, or without pieces of their legs, or whether a spider's head could function without the spider, or whether cockroach wings were capable of an orphaned flight. He could have advanced science if the desire to understand hadn't been replaced too soon by the dark taste for cutting. The age of the blade was also the bane of the earthworms, whose obstination to live in scattered pieces puzzled him, and that of the dragonflies, captured on the clotheslines where the families hung their laundry to dry on sunny days.

The hour of the dragonfly precedes that of the sun. It accompanies the dew—an evanescent unction that seeps from the earth (no one sees it fall) and covers the world in glittering drops. The little boy noted this mystery when a desire to follow Ma Ninotte, off on an urgent morning mission, propelled him from his bed before dawn. Through the window in the hall, from which the inner courtyard, the tubs, and the roofs of the kitchens were visible, he saw the sky and the top of the wall, crowned with grass growing from nothing, pensive shrubs, and minuscule flowers. And it all appeared varnished beneath the rising of the barely warm sun, the wind circulating sea scents and nocturnal secrets. He breathed them in as if taking them into his open spirit, these wonders that for him were the sole structures of the world. One of the most beautiful wonders were the dragonflies. How was it possible that a city, before its heat, could inspire such immobile grace in the wind, so much glittering finesse, ocher reflections, green reflections, silent and secret life that vanished with the slap of the sun? Straight shiny wings visible when at rest and big eyes, velvety and matte, almost melancholy. Oh, how the dragonflies worshiped the drops! On the reflective puddles they quivered, dripped, celebrated mass for the water like desert travelers remembering their longest thirst. After capturing them and cutting off everything possible, the little boy adopted their ways. Anointing himself priest of their ceremony, he developed a taste for honoring the dew like a secret of the nocturnal humors of the earth and the sky. Certain dragonflies whispered to him that to this august mixture had to be added the tear of a star, but he never went for it, not because he didn't believe it but because it wasn't good, he believed, for a priest to seem to swallow the foolishness of his flock, even if they were, as he concluded at the end of his day-dreams, absolutely right.

A cloud of dragonflies (frequently) announced a day of steady westerly winds and of fine rain. The roof of the building being no longer very hearty, Ma Ninotte accompanied these watery days with the catch-as-catch-can plan, intended to save the apartment from flooding. First there were two tubs positioned in the living room, one next to the buffet that was losing its varnish, the other beneath one of the two windows whose weak joints permitted drops of water to descend, at first hesitantly, then almost continuously, as the rain stretched into eternity. The ceiling darkened with rings, limited here and there by patches of paint still fresh from the New Year's coat. The walls of the facade, quickly soaked, released a glossy, oozing substance that had to be collected in rags on the floor. The ceiling of the bedroom whose windows overlooked the street was, in and of itself, a catastrophe. It required so many tubs, rags, pots, pans, glasses, and sometimes even umbrellas that Ma Ninotte had hung up a large oilcloth. She had connected it with a string from the Syrians to nails planted in the four corners of the room. During the inclement weather the little boy, abandoning the staircase and the kitchen roofs, contemplated the progressive curve of the oilcloth beneath the weight of a pool of water. Yellowish at the start, as it aged the water thus collected tended toward chicken-caca brown. During the rainy months Ma Ninotte didn't empty the sheet: the operation was delicate, dangerous, and difficult. It demanded a concentration that this warrior negress, in her perpetual struggle with life, applied to other emergencies. The water stagnated in its plastic chalice, growing blacker as the rains and days passed. In the warm weather that followed, its evaporation left a dusty, blackish residue, a most unglamorous setting for the slightly discolored chips of paint.

Thus, at the start of each rain, Ma Ninotte, followed by her little boy, inspected the kitchen, the dining room, and the two bedrooms, verifying the placement of the tubs, the dampness of the rags, the resistance of the oilcloth. Sometimes she leaned out the window to estimate the length of the downpour ("A-a fout la pli-a ka fésé ko'y jodi-a!"), then returned to her cooking without worrying unduly about the sky's charades. Anastasia, the older of the two sisters, went to warm her bed in the company of a doll made by Ma Ninotte in days of destitution. She didn't play with it anymore but couldn't live without it. A tall *câpresse-chabine* with big hair, it was she who took command when Ma Ninotte wasn't around. Her long hands were so tapered as to make the slightest rap painful. To transgress her dictates was a sign of temporary insanity. Her authority was invincible; she had inherited from Ma Ninotte an aptitude for conquering life, for foreseeing everything, for knowing everything, for organizing everything, to such an extent that Papa (French-language spinner and Master of the Art of the Creole nickname) called her "the Baroness." The second sister was Marielle, a kind of dark, vaguely Indian-looking *câpresse,* a champion in the ancient art of competition basketball, who lost herself in photonovels and in books without pictures. This one (Papa had nicknamed her "Choune") seemed to live outside the house, outside the world, regulating her life as a function of demands whose clock was at the center of herself. According to her, we were called upon to live according to our hearts, to do or not do as we pleased, the only rules being never to sleep on her bed or to touch her comb or her belongings. Steady in mood, maybe even blasé, she remained difficult to surprise or to interest. The first of the two older brothers (called "Jojo" by Father the nicknamer) remained, during the rain (and the rest of the time as well), seated at the table in the dining room. In the midst of a cluster of books and notebooks, he waged a continual war against algebraic formulas. He covered hundreds of pages with them, scattered here-there-and-everywhere. Each of us picked one up on occasion to experience the anguish of confronting these senseless signs on which the genius (otherwise indifferent) adolescent seemed to confer all power for explaining the world. The second older brother, Paul, ever at war with the Baroness, sat on the stairs at the end of the hall, right in front of the widow Ma Romulus's landing. There, his head between his knees, transistor to his ear, he fell into a kind of rhythmic hypnosis in which only his toes and fingers seemed alive. He was a fellow who explained the world through music, but he seemed to have lost his ear for the melody of the rains. He had put together a guitar that produced sounds via horsehair threads. And these sounds sufficed for him to leave the earth and head for places known to him alone, places filled with an intoxicating oxygen. This gave him the opaque look of visionaries and a similar lack of aptitude for washing the dishes. In fact — the Baroness finally had to admit — the child was a musician.

Troubled by the silent struggle between the oilcloth and the aerial pond, the little boy lay down beneath it, on Ma Ninotte's big bed, provided Papa wasn't taking his nap. He stared at the yellowish lump that grew heavier, both afraid and impatient to see it break under the weight. He imagined, full of fright and delectation, the hard shower that would almost knock him out. Sometimes he climbed on a chair to tickle the oilcloth with the tip of his finger. The plastic always seemed too weak, and the shower imminent. So he climbed back down quickly, feverishly, to lie directly beneath it.

All the apartments were subject to the same inconveniences. The house was as old as eternity, it seems: the little boy never met anyone with a memory long enough to recall a time of splendor. He always wondered, for example, what the initial paint—which no one remembered—had been like. At his birth there subsisted a color of indefinable chemistry, chipped according to its relations with the sun, a source of dust and of a slightly vinegary odor. During dry spells it looked like remnants of ash. In the rain the air filled with woodsy smells, and the enigmatic paint, saturated with dampness, took on a grayish, velvety or rough, hue. It then became nourishment for a mass of insects, which emerged from somewhere—frightened by the rain, exalted by the rain—and spent their fearful moments running through the walls, which turned into a playful breeding ground.

Ma Ninotte and Ma Romulus were the biggest busybodies. They sometimes took it upon themselves to describe the unpleasantries of the rain to the Syrian, the owner of the apartments. In their presence the latter took refuge in a quasi-cataleptic meditation. Only his lip, stretched around a fine cigar, indicated that he was still there. Ma Ninotte and Ma Romulus, baffled, forgot their rage. And when the Syrian, suddenly resuscitating, bid them farewell for the umpteenth time ("Okay, well, I'll have a look at it soon"), they never dreamed of reacting as they had imagined a thousand times they would: sending the mountains of fabrics flying, grabbing his bush shirt by the collar, telling him to his face (as they said behind his back): "La Syrie siguine siguine andièt!"

They returned somber, willing themselves reassured anyway. To Ma Irénée, who awaited the news on her doorstep, they reported in stereo: "The Syrian said he's going to have a look at it soon." And the house went back to normal: the shuddering wood rotted by water, the crackling of tin beneath the seasonal downpours, the chanting of Negresses before their dangerous stoves, the smell of cooked sugar, the chattering, the radios tuned in until the batteries wore out, and the sudden stampeding of children rushing to sit at the bottom of the stairs, facing the street, and who, half an hour later, launched into another stampede, only to sit down again at the top, drunk with the racket they made on the wooden steps. Their ascents and descents were so regular that Ma Romulus behind her Singer, Ma Irénée in her kitchen salting her fries, Ma la Sirène with her rosary, and Ma Ninotte struggling with her pots and pans were able to keep close track of time. If not for that, from August to November, between the drops, the rings, the tubs, the rags, and the Syrian's meditations, time would stand still.

Once, I vaguely remember, the Syrian dispatched a carpenter to repair the roofs. This bitter black man lugged his tools in a soft leather bag. He entered the house with the look of not quite believing the pupils of his eyes. He used his toe to gauge the somewhat tired strength of the stairs. Observing the assemblage and planks and beams (impeccable carpentry work, of an ancient science that has already been collectively lost), he grumbled: "Joy bel kay!" What a house! while remaining appalled that anyone, in these times of rains, fires, and cyclones, could persist in living in something other than a cement blockhouse. The black man, he explained, had already done his time in straw huts, then in wood huts, then in asbestos cement huts. . . . Given his predisposition for being wiped off the surface of this earth, those types of houses were never really the Good Lord's blessings. He had read in some philosophical work some business about little pigs, and he explained to Ma Romulus (who wasn't even impressed) that cement was the bearer not only of the future but also of a finer way of life. A carpenter by chance, today he was a cementer by vocation, that is to say, out of a sense of the modern and a vision of the future. And he concluded: The only little pig that escaped the wolf had built a house of cement. "What wolf are you talking about?" gnashed Ma Romulus. "There ain't no wolves here!" "It was an allegory," he responded, "you can substitute a snake." "I've never seen a snake eat a pig," protested Ma Ninotte. The carpenter, distressed, stopped trying to converse with so much ignorance and pulled out his professional pencil. Each family explained to him its miseries, showed him the leaks, the rings, the swellings of the walls, each one gave him an accounting of liters per week and of drops per second. He listened with an air of comprehension. Then he went up to the attic to access the roof.

The opening was located in the hallway, smack in front of Ma Irénée's door. He raised the hatch and, before the stupefied boy, forsook his ladder for the dark space beneath the tin. There was a silence before the agony. The carpenter began to scream, then to whimper, then to curse a colony of things that were scratching him, biting him, raising around him a hoopla of dust. He descended head first and began running, uttering a rare malediction. He returned some time later, pressed by the Syrian, and took care to evacuate ancient toothless cats, twenty-two bats, and a passel of rats not so nasty as all that. Then he got to working, installing new tin sheets, filling in others, repairing the gutters. One could see him hanging from the edge of the facade, without even a rope to close his tomb, working with a what-do-I-care attitude until the job was done. At noon, he remained in the attic. We could hear him regaling himself alone, naming each of his mouthfuls: "Hmm cod, hmm red beans, hmm peppers." He refused all invitations but wasn't above accepting the bits of fried fish hoisted up through the trap door. When he left, we awaited the next rainfall with anxious computations, bets, and numerous evaluations. When it came, nothing very new occurred: the house still leaked, but not in the same places, and it took everyone some time to readjust the tubs beneath this diluvian revenge.

For the Prime Confidante, this story is all rubbish. There was never the slightest rat beneath the tin roof, nor the slightest cat; at most there might have been two or three bats, judging by the soaring of a twilight wing. But that could just as easily have been the sound of a zombi. And when the carpenter went up to the attic there were no problems, and the proof of his incompetence is that he was able to work at his ease. "Too bad if it's a lie," argues the shameful scribe.

"It's not too bad, it's a lie," she responds, unwavering.

The house lived with the rain, but during the dry season—oh, what a time!—it vibrated. Everything became breakable, the wood fought with the nails to snatch a little more space. The beams wanted to descend to catch the rare wind through the windows. The planks of the halls and the walls, finding themselves with sap once again, creaked with nastic movement. The overheated tin afflicted life like a heavy hat. Upon contact with breezes it became musical, like the sound of bottles on the verge of breaking. Then, from each fiber of the ceiling, a dust emerged, the finest, the grayest, the most persistent of dusts. The house shed a skin during the heat. It emerged from this molting noisy as a crate of crabs, slightly more austere, less pensive, and most of all foreign. An unyielding light accentuated the zones of shadow. The area below the stairs became a vast hole where scarcely a murderous imagination dared venture. From the interior window slanted a hot light that projected the corridor into the nonexistence of an impenetrable blackness. And it was like that everywhere, entirely erased, or entirely exploding. Our lives got stuck in zigzags of light, of opaque torpor, overcome with a stupor evidenced only by interminable siestas and the inhabitual silence of a dehydrated pack of kids—Lord, what a time!

During the dry season we lived differently. Without speaking of heat, we lived the heat. The mothers moved with urgency before dawn, slackening their pace upon the rising of the sun. Their pupils drooped beneath a slower lid. They seemed to freshen their worries of survival, smatterings of a dream, and their occasionally drowned gazes gave evidence of an interior abyss in which they took refuge (no doubt a place bathed in former loves: the only water-for-thirst possible in this living oven). Long hair went up to aerate the nape of the neck. The madras kerchiefs, unraveled by idle hands, fanned asphyxiated faces. The large-skirted dresses lifted to the hips, the simple cotton shifts (fine, white, vaporous) emerged from forgotten suitcases, in which one rediscovered—despite the mothballs and the knots of good leaves—the destruction of subterranean cockroaches or, worse, nests of pink mice. These horrifying discoveries produced the best orchestras of the season. A call went out for the death of the rodents who, too clever to show themselves, forced us to laugh. We never spoke of heat; we lived it. It meant speaking less loudly and, no doubt, for less long. Song stitched only the dawn, and evenings were livelier. People went to catch the sunset from their window ledges, in a Fort-de-France that soothed the day's heat rash in the lazy breeze of the evening dew. No one spoke of the heat. But we learned to live differently in the house, to keep the shutters shut around the remnants of the night, to open them at the rising of a breeze, to live in the air currents while remaining wary of them. In the streets, you had to know where the shade was and the map of the fresh winds. Only people from the country and tourists sweat like pigs before tall shop windows. Not a word about the heat, as if to negate the heat.

Because he couldn't cover himself, the heat exposed the little boy to the mosquitos of the night. At the price of scratches and anemic insomnias, he had to mow them down in flight, with a hand as quick as the shadow of a yellow snake. Informed of the slightest landing on his skin, a special sense, born of necessity, triggered swats that were fatal for the tiny beasts and painful for him, but which constituted revenge for the cunning buzz-buzzings in the depth of his ear. You had to be as patient as the mosquito itself, wait-for-it, listen-for-it, calculate its arrival, then swat at the blackness and the quivering of a wing. Sometimes there were twenty-twelve thousand of them. The little boy then took refuge under his sheet, a sweatbox akin to hell and useless to boot: certain well-equipped mosquitos pierced the thin cloth. When he learned that mosquitos feared the wind, he cut a collection of cardboard pieces from Italian shoeboxes and, as soon as night fell, fanned himself nonstop, positively churning up the air. The tiny vampires kept their distance, defeated by their very weightlessness. A fine victory, but he had to learn to sleep while continuing his fanning motion. It's possible he succeeded, but no one has ever come forth as a witness.

What predominates is the memory of impatience. A supreme impatience based on the anticipation of some kind of completion, of some particular knowledge capable of giving meaning to what he is, to the powerless state in which he finds himself—powerless with regard to grownups, with regard to the mysteries of the world, a vast powerlessness vis-à-vis himself, which he masks by projecting the insouciance of a child. He is pleased to see the days go by, and the hours never pass quickly enough. The rising sun is one big promise, and night, which he always resists, must conquer his lids. They then grow heavier than the world, fearful of light, dusty, fluttering. At that point nothing can be done but dissolve into the obligatory prayers to the Virgin and into dreams without memories. He falls off quickly and is invincible. Sometimes his energy slackens into an immobility to which the gang of children is accustomed. It's something that is triggered neither by time nor a feeling, but a kind of stoppage inside himself, a silent waiting in which empty dreams take over and the brain turns into stale foliage, full of expectant birdlike fevers. The melancholy boy then knows the world and silently questions his life (it was a matter, I believe, of a child's unexpressed anxiety; but it is also possible that these were simply hours of stupor connected to the idiocy of which certain other little boys — his very closest enemies — suspected him).

The site of these immobilizations was the kitchen roofs. The house possessed an interior courtyard, narrow and deep, which wrapped around the back of the house. In this courtyard, the families shared two or three tubs for laundry. Opposite, against the wall, were the kitchens: little wood rooms with cement floors and tin roofs, each containing a coal stove in which the food was cooked. This separation of the kitchen from the house, which is very Creole, aimed to protect the house in case of fire. The little boy never saw the day when the mothers cooked side by side in these rooms, separated by wood dividers. He never saw the coal-lighting ceremonies or those for maintaining an eternal ember. He never saw the pots of inexhaustible soup, complemented, depending on finances, with a beef bone, a marrow, or a bag of vegetables. Over time these soups mutated into a mangrove swamp of tastes, able to fuel everyone's energies (both those with teeth and those without). He imagines the disturbingly spicy steam that pervaded these rooms where the mamas showed the world their culinary talents. They competed in audacity in order to scent the pickled fish, send wafting odoriferous fricassees, better transmit to the universe that there was, in their part of the world, on that day, not a miserable cod sauce, but a slice of beef. He supposes that they also sang, or chatted through the dividers, before hauling their big pots up the creaking stairs to a pack of starving children, home from school, and to the men busy drinking punch in the company of the midday boozer, expert in timing his visit.

The use of the outdoor kitchens entailed numerous risks, reveals the Prime Confidante. One's peppers disappeared. So-and-so needed oil and generously helped herself. To lose a piece of meat was not uncommon if you were called upstairs by some emergency. The thieves were cats or other beings more or less close to humanity. One mumbled curses against them for months on end, accusing them without ever naming them or mentioning their resemblance to such or such a neighbor, for "it's true that the nigger will always be a nigger and that—when hard up—Negresses and dogs are quick to burn you."

By the time the little boy came along, the kitchens were dead. They served as storehouses for things whose utility became apparent only with the urgencies of misfortune. Certain families used them as washrooms. Grownups spent many soapy, song-filled hours there. Ma Ninotte, it seems, was the first to transform her kitchen into a chicken coop. This no doubt occurred on the occasion of the visit of some countrywoman doing her annual city rounds. The latter must have shown up in her starched calico, stocked according to tradition with herbs-for-every-ill, with yams and, no doubt, with two little chicks picked up in the forest. Ma Ninotte had placed her chicks in the kitchen, fed them on corn and a dusting of gingerbread. Once the little ones had grown, she must have served them at a festive Sunday dinner, with baptismal vermouth and a bouquet of fresh flowers filling the house with perfume. It must have been a pleasant affair, and, come Monday morning, Ma Ninotte probably inquired after two more chicks.

Another version of the genesis of the chicken coops is possible. Ma Ninotte, who was raised in the country, seeing that the space was left empty, probably envisioned what any country woman faced with the demands of urban survival would have seen: either a garden or a chicken coop. Since the site was cemented, the idea of a chicken coop must have won out. Papa probably pleaded in vain: "Dear Gros-Kato,* is it reasonable, in the middle of an urban metropolis?" But Ma Ninotte, whose will was on the order of a cyclone's, must have arrived at the Lamentin early one Sunday to gather a few chicks from their swampy meanderings. So that by the time the little boy came along, several hens were already clucking in the old kitchen. The other families did the same, but only as circumstances required. Ma Ninotte, however, possessed a permanent chicken coop that never fell below two cocks and six or seven hens. And that's why the rats became intolerable.

Fort-de-France, at that time, had not yet declared war on rats. Along with the crabs, the latter inhabited the Levassor Canal, crumbled sidewalks, and other well-covered waterways. They haunted the gullies. They scoured the city in subterranean fashion. They emerged in the nocturnal refuse and accompanied the insomniac stroll of lunar poets. A colony of them padded about in the staircase of the house. Absorbed with his spiders, his cockroaches, and his dragonflies, the little boy didn't notice them right away. A few squeaks here and there. A fleeting shadow in the canal. But during one of his moments of stillness on the roof of the kitchens, he discovered the fabulous spectacle. Here's how.

At about one in the afternoon, Fort-de-France became lethargic, with fewer pedestrians and fewer horns. Country people sought refuge in the shade to eat. The Syrians lowered the metal curtains of their shops. The dust of this urban desert began to flutter. Behind the house, on the roof of the kitchens, a shadow offered its cool haven to the little boy. On Saturday afternoons the languor deepened. Certain families went off to the country, to mass, to catechism, or to take care of some other business.

*Creole name meaning Polaris, the polestar — PC

Finally, the house creaked under the weight of silence, and the little boy was free to grow still. It was on a day like that when . . . a squeak lifted him out of his inner emptiness, calling him to the edge of the roof. That's when he saw the rats, down in the courtyard. Five or six, yes, scourers searching for crumbs, tub climbers, tightrope artists on the edge of buckets, disappearing into the kitchens and reappearing just as fast. Very young rats and very old rats. Others, fearful, emerged from the covered canal only to pounce on a tidbit of food.

The little boy believed he was discovering an obscure life form that paralleled that of the house. The rats had already—though he didn't know it at the time—caught the attention of the adults. This would become apparent to him only with the arrival of Ma Ninotte's laying hens, whose eggs the rats carted off with a never-before-seen ingenuity. In the absence of eggs, they slayed the chicks by the dozen (and the half dozen). The massacres were discovered at dawn, before the arrival of the water, and Ma Ninotte shrieked the foulest of morning maledictions. The chicks had been half devoured and some of the hens wounded by these little sharp-toothed beasts. Poison in tiny pink packets was deployed, which decimated them in threes and fours, then became ineffectual. The mouse traps (soaped, sprinkled with disinfectant, scented with fresh meat) attracted no rat after the first usage. So the campaign lost steam, the diminished colony was forgotten, and, until the next massacre of chicks and the death cry sounded by Ma Ninotte, we endured the misery of a staircase swarming with an invisible ratly life form.

After noticing these creatures, the little boy developed a special extermination plan of his own. He would have been perfectly incapable of explaining why, but his discovery of the world first provoked this perhaps comforting reflex to kill. Among the rats there was one that was older than the others; slower, more wary, but powerful and more cunning. He ventured into the open

Feeling 25

only under conditions of optimal security, against a backdrop of pure silence. Not until the floorboards of the house had stopped moving, and Fort-de-France, shut down, gave in to the dust, did the old rat appear, risking his shadow beneath the vertical heel of the sun, making the game worth the candle. He was massive, peeled, and stitched with scars; he had lost an ear, a piece of his tail, and perhaps also some part of himself that made him no longer just a rat. He was so experienced it was terrifying; his heart didn't leap at every puff of wind, but his finely tuned ear and acute eye told him when to disappear instantly. He had no habits, never passed the same spot twice, and never retreated in the same manner. This was the rat that the little boy chose — go figure! — as his very first victim.

A strange relationship developed. It lasted an unspecified period of time and fizzled out without any resolution. The boy found himself a string and created a slipknot, which he laid out in the courtyard. In the middle he set down a piece of sausage. With the knot wedged in place, the string in his fist, he sat at his lookout on the roof. The idea was to lasso the vicious old rat. But the animal must have disliked sausage, or else the sight of the lasso cast him into a strategic melancholy that kept him in his hole, philosophizing about some dark rat affairs. Whatever the case, he never showed up. It was always another, younger, stupider rat who ventured into the slipknot and lunged for the sausage. The little boy pulled with all his might. He must have pulled a thousand-twelve-thousand times before accepting the impossibility of catching a rat with a sausage-lasso setup. The knot closed around itself and the impatient boy hauled up nothing but a dangling string.

His next contraption was a basin weighted down by a rock. A piece of wood connected to an invisible string held it in the air. The old rat (he never turned up) was supposed to venture underneath in order to collect the bait. Those who did risk it raced off with the sausage, as if alerted to the trapper's intentions. At other, rarer times they fled empty-mouthed. Afterward not a single one returned. There was the flaming gourd, the infernal jar, the superglue, the rubber band, the guillotine knife, the poison syrup, the terrifying scissors of doom. . . . But even this arsenal of small cruelties was not enough to snare the slightest hint of rat. Too late he learned that he would have had to remove his smell from the traps, never reuse a bait, avoid presenting a dubious windfall within tooth's reach. It took him some time to understand that, in fact, rats were smart.

One day the old rat spotted him. Standing on the edge of the tub, he furtively glanced his way, then pursued his quest. Two inhuman orbs of opaque blackness served as his eyes. For a split second these eyes brushed over him and, in a certain sense, scorned him. Never again did the old rat, even though he knew the boy to be watching, grant him a second glance. He modified his routes and always remained far from the overhang of the roof where the little boy—changing his tactics, trying to be selective—was perched, rock in hand, directly above the bait on the ground, waiting to crush the Old Man's back.

Hours of lookout were required, the rock held in his outstretched arm above the void: lying on the tin roof, watching with only one eye, hoping for silence, breathing in calmness, turning to rust in order to melt into the roof, praying for the old rat to approach, and ignoring the other rats nibbling the bait. Toward the end, however, his stiffened arms would drop the vengeful rock on frenzied latecomers, but even these speedy creatures avoided being crushed, with leaps that became increasingly leisurely. Their losses beneath the far-too-slow-moving stone never amounted to more than a snippet of tail, a tuft of hair. Around these measly trophies the little boy organized pagan ceremonies. The man clutches them today somewhere in his shadows.

Feeling 27

The old rat disappeared sometimes, not to be seen for several weeks. The little boy supposed him dead of old age. He imagined secret cemeteries visited by night, situated at the very heart of thick wood posts. He imagined the streets of Fort-de-France covered with these exhausted rats who knew their way around poison and who, suddenly hearing some obscure call, would set out to dig a grave with their last tooth. He imagined his aging adversary, a rat isolated by his years: so much intelligence, such cunning, such caution, so much genius—all ending in dirty dereliction, with no address other than death and forgetting. So the little boy arranged funerals for him on tiny cars. A box of matches served as a coffin. The procession traveled the hallway, informing the bugs of the walls, and ended in a liturgy he improvised himself, in rat language. A burial concluded this ceremony in a hole gouged in the wall near the stairs, where a brick released from its plaster delivered its redness to a burrowing nail. The little boy would go away melancholy, missing his old friend, until one day he would see him reappear. Then, rather than rejoicing, he would dash off to invent some atrocity capable of finishing him off, this time for real.

He watched him grow old. It was nothing: a stiffness in the back, a misshapen silhouette, the constant shaking of an ear. He was horrified to see him linger beneath a risk, react sometimes a touch slowly. He caught him nibbling things he had scoffed at before and stand too often immobile, distracted in a senile sort of way. He watched him fall apart. It was nothing: a feeling of pity that rose upon seeing him. No longer the desire to kill him, only the horror of a benign commiseration. The little boy often had the impression that if he came down from the roof, the Old Man would wait for him and allow himself to be touched.

One day, the Old Man limped toward the bait that lay beneath the rock that the boy still brandished, out of habit, from the heights of his lookout. He advanced with a kind of blind—or desperate or absent-minded—faith, something on the order of a suicidal impulse or the sense that he had little to lose. His diminishing strength allowed him no more than this tiny windfall. He stepped into the trap and began chewing like a church cockroach at the moment of the Host. The stone did not crush his skull: it had become the keystone of a cathedral of pity in the child, who wept.

O selective memory. You no longer remember his disappearance. In which attic did you store his death? Did you see him floating belly-up in the courtyard tub, or do you retain a vision of his hunched body on one of the steps? Do you remember him emerging into the daylight, his brain shipwrecked without a compass, standing bewildered beneath the mamas' brooms? It's possible he never died, that he simply decided to change houses. I can't picture him dead, floating in the mucky stream of a canal. Perhaps he set up camp between two dreams and remains there, mummified in an eternal insomnia. Memory, that is my decision.

There is no precise date, no period when the rats were definitively abandoned. No cutoff point or moment of disinterest but the progressive loss of astonishment, a silent complicity, without familiarity and without an ounce of sympathy. The rats became one of the world's possibilities, the oldest among them serving as a banner—and a symbol of variation from the norm. They transformed the little boy's nature. Beneath the killer lay the makings of someone who today is incapable of doing the slightest harm to the most despicable of the green flies. This sentimentality would in fact complicate the life of Ma Ninotte: she began to have trouble killing her hens and her pink-eyed rabbits, but most of all, her pigs.

After the chicks Ma Ninotte launched into the pig business. By some fluke a little pig appeared in the former kitchen turned chicken coop. It had to coexist with the hens for a time before Ma Ninotte would grant its kind the entire site. They were skinny little *cochons-planches* that we fattened the entire year, in keeping with the rural philosophy. They were destined for the Christmas feast, a singsong time filled with sausages, chops, patés, stews, and roasts. They were fed on leftovers, green bananas, useless words, nicknames; they scarfed down the seasonal fruit peels, and the children lavished a kindly tenderness on them. Some were perfumed, adorned with hats, necklaces, lace. Others enjoyed the pleasure of being scratched on the sides and belly for days on end. Sometimes they escaped from the kitchen, which had become a pig parking lot, and dashed into the street, followed by our mob and the valiant step of Ma Ninotte. We caught them in less than an hour with the help of some resourceful fellow or a countrywoman capable of immobilizing pigs by calling out a single old word. This was a common phenomenon. At that time, Fort-de-France was home to the country; in the streets were mules, horses, Puerto Rican oxen headed for the slaughterhouse, ducks flying headless, scattered chickens, goats that had broken away from an Indian sacrifice, tame birds, and dogs meandering with a bodyful of scars. So everyone knew how to corner a pig. Ma Ninotte's only fear as she ran after her own was that it would be stolen, but as I write this, I suddenly remember that nothing at the time was stolen. Everyone knew the factor of survival offered by the slightest pig to entire families. A pig on the lam received unanimous respect. If Ma Ninotte was worried, it was probably that this precious treasure would expire beneath the wheel of a car, thus compromising the Christmas to come. I remember the pigs; they were called Mouse, Matador, Tio-Tio, Héliazord, Master Popol, River-Sausage; they loved us with their eyes and in human ways. Their flights were like ritual races that once a year brought excitement to their reclusive lives on death row.

Some years were hard. Despite all the food it received, the pig remained as thin as the shadow of a strand of hair. Ma Ninotte augmented its portions with cow milk, then in despair consulted the country experts who came down to do business in the market. They examined the animal's eyes, the thickness of its coat, the color of its tongue. They considered the diameter of its dejections, and it always ended in a ritual accusation against worms. The pig then spent its days ingurgitating tufts of cleansing flowers and yellowish herbs that unclogged the intestines. Ma Ninotte mixed its food, on a moonlit night, with rare oils concentrated in witches' gourds. The pig then expelled a part of its soul, most of its memories, sickly humors, and invisible worms. But (and this was the main thing), it began to get better, it was obliged to get better, which is to say, to preserve around its ribs a first layer of fat, and then a second, not to mention that its flesh developed a density that Ma Ninotte patted every day in anticipation of the joy of her next Christmas.

Other times the pig degenerated despite all the attention. The diagnosis was then clear: it had been tainted with an old curse, a power of those blacks jealous of others' possessions. Suffering in those days always had an origin; nothing went unexplained, except perhaps happiness, but that was so rare. Between the hand of the Good Lord, the interventions of the Holy Virgin, the appearances of an infinite number of patron saints, and the curses passed down by a long line of the envious, there was no misfortune in the world that could not be broken with a load of prayers or some baths in healthy leaves — and this was mighty convenient. We bathed the pig and recited over it. The baths were given by Ma Ninotte, but the recitations were spoken by some old Negro from far away and from whom the children were kept at a distance. The man had a gentle voice and confident gestures; there was something reassuring and disturbing about him at the same time from which the pig always benefited by putting on some good fat. But those years of skinny-pigs were not as frequent as pebbles on the paths, and they became rare after the comet passed.

The little boy did not become equally attached to every pig. They were different. Some turned out to be more engaging than others, more lively, more mischievous, more capable of affection. In our shared memory, brothers, there was Matador. He arrived a bag of rattling bones and developed into a charming monster who laughed at the world with the eyes of an elder. He gave the impression of feeding seven times off the slightest scrap. He loved chocolate, soap, loving scratches, and Creole songs; he welcomed his visitors with a nod of the head and stretched an attentive ear toward the sound of our voices. His escape into the city was one of the worst, for his weight made him a rolling boulder. The helpful fellow of the day, seeking to corner him, found himself flying toward the wire of an electric pole. The others, hanging on to Matador's coat, were driven into the gutters as if their shirts had been caught in a propeller. When Ma Ninotte, followed by her brat pack, caught up with them, the victims asked her: "Tell us, ma'am, what seventh species of animal is this, if you please?" Others, who'd toppled over, feet in the air, drew up an indictment: He's a public danger number thirty-three (the age of Christ's death), he's a sower of booboos, a liver boiler, a pian skinner, a toothache stabber, a body crusher, a rheumatism starter, a filth maker, and if you don't mind my saying so, Mrs. So-and-so, an ill-bred bastard of a beast . . ." They rounded up Matador on the banks of the Pointe Simon, opposite the white man's warehouses, where he had stopped to unceremoniously suck down the scrumptious emanations of a salted-meat barrel.

The killer was a certain Marcel, a dog dressed as a man, who seemed to exist only as Christmas approached, when he became a pig slaughterer. We had become so attached to Matador that the fellow was welcomed with cries of hatred. The man, who ordinarily never took off his hat, raised it to scratch a reminiscence of hair. He'd brought no implements; he had come, as he did every year, to agree on a price, a day, and a time, and if it was difficult every year, the year of Matador was a real ordeal for him. As December approached, Ma Ninotte faced a parade of sniveling delegations imploring grace. To which she responded with a feigned (and desperate) rage (for she loved Matador as much as we did): "Ti-anmay soti en zèb mwen!" Get away from my feet, you brats! For her to keep a pig was impossible, unthinkable, as we later learned, once we had decoded the tables of survival in the city. Sensing extraordinary difficulty to come in the case of Matador, she hid all preparations. We never saw her buy the peppers, nor the sack of onions, nor the coarse salt, nor the herbs that announced the evil Saturday of the fattened pig. The only giveaway was Marcel.

He arrived by day in his white visiting shirt, beneath the hat that camouflaged his long-gone hair. As usual, he called up from the first step: "Ma Ninotte, how'd the pig do this year?" To which only our horde responded. And not politely. In those days the Creole language had ample resources when it came to insults. It fascinated us, as it did all the children, by its ability to contest (in two or three words, an onomatopoeia, a suction noise, twelve rapid tongue twisters about the mamas or the genitals) the French order that governed speech. It was as if it had hardened around that which could not be spoken, where proper language lost its footing in the swampylands of feelings. It enabled us to exist furiously, aggressively, in an iconoclastic, roundabout way. There was mutiny in the language. The children possessed a joyful intuition about it and tested it in secret, positioning themselves opposite the grownups in the particular matrix of this suffocated tongue. That is why, despite (and especially thanks to) the situation of domination, the Creole language is a fine playground for childhood frustrations and exerts an underground impact on the psychic structure that is inaccessible to the established elevations of the French tongue. I don't know if Marcel appreciated this quality, but in any case he must have understood deep down what we were telling him. Eying us like a pack of zombis, he took cover in the shelter of Ma Ninotte. We watched him from afar coming to an understanding over punch. It was awful. He left amid the mortal silence imposed by the presence of Ma Ninotte by his side. But he must have felt our hatred in the curves of our backs, the rolling of our eyes, the disdainful folds of our lips, the way we eyed him up and down, all this mimed spittle that the Creole language carries in its silent orations.

Crying was not a matter of tears, but a tilling of the body through the socket of the tear duct. It wasn't two tears, but a heart drowning, weighing heavy in the chest.

Then began a long wait, o brothers, the most terrible, I believe, of our collective childhoods. December arrived, its winds, its cold drafts, swollen noses, upset stomachs, fitful coughs, and old flu. The evenings were loaded with colors, and the days laid their tints on the changing lights, soft suns, rains often streaked with luminous clouds. We remained vigilant. We counted the knives and the tubs, but Ma Ninotte seemed to be preparing a pigless Christmas. She tended to the peels of her orange liqueur. She prettied her salted ham, her preserves, the other delicacies she accumulated in her cupboard while awaiting the days of joy. We never heard her promise anyone the slightest chop, and no one passed on a little note from some lady-next-door who habitually received a lean pound or two. Nothing. Christmas approached, rich in its evening hymns, which began on the radio and reverberated among us on the stairs. Only Matador sensed his fate. He could have told us, had we learned to read his eyes, decode his grunts, understand the listlessness that came from the vague prescience of his fate.

Marcel must have set to work in the middle of the night and arranged to be far away by the time we awoke, leaving us a whitish, bloody mass in place of Matador, a mass that Ma Ninotte cut up with her broad-bladed knife and distributed in newspaper as gifts to the families of the house, to the doctor who cured us, to the pharmacist who gave her medicines, to the Syrians who helped her out of jams. The rest was for her, in the form of cured meats, roasts, chops, pig's head, and sausages, which we had neither the stomach nor the heart to eat. I'm talking about, if not a bitter Christmas, then at least a somber one.

Memory, I see your game: you take root and form in the imagination, and the latter blossoms only through you.

I have no memory of the pigs that succeeded Matador. Suffering is a harsh vaccine. It must have prepared us not to get attached to Christmas pigs. The others must have passed through in an atmosphere of relative indifference, a little as the already burnt throat is indifferent to the passing of the rum. All I remember of the pigs was Christmas — not a religious Christmas, but an unusually generous life, one that doled out a little tolerance. We could shout, sing, eat plenty of sweets, go to bed late, ask for stories. The hallway that linked up the families was inhabited into the blackest of the night. The mamas welcomed guests and prepared and prepared and prepared the next day's feast. The air was trimmed with scents from the cake ovens, the steam of fricassees, the porous cork of blissful liqueurs poured for us over fat cubes of ice. Ma Ninotte moved at a different pace. For her, as for the other negresses struggling for survival, the year that was coming to an end had been conquered, its store of miseries beaten. They could gather up its debris with the dust of the house and cast them out together to make way for fresh hopes.

This time of the year includes a special ceremony: the preparation of the manger.

At a time unknown to the little boy, Anastasia the Baroness, the older of the two sisters, had suffered from the absence of a manger. Ma Ninotte and Papa's purses weren't full enough to erect the illuminated cave of the Savior the way everyone else did, in the middle of the living room. Anastasia pleaded for a manger with big tears. These tears touched Ma Ninotte, who erased the sadness. She taught the child how to sculpt in used candle wax. Anastasia launched into it with an artfulness and a patience whose secret lay in necessity. With the melted candles she made herself a donkey, an ox, a Virgin Mary, a Joseph, shepherds, Magi Kings, a star, and, of course, a baby Savior. With a sooty brush she drew their eyes and ears, smiles and feelings, styles and mannerisms. She placed them all on some dried grass and crumpled a hieroglyphic cave of newspaper around them. She had her manger. To top it all off, she added two lighted candles, which had a beautiful effect but calamitous consequences. The shepherds began to melt. The donkey and the ox formed a puddle. The Virgin Mary melded with Joseph, who was swallowed up by the Magi Kings. Very quickly the manger became a catastrophic grayish blob, sending Anastasia into the worst kind of childhood distress. Subsequently the episode has been mentioned so often that the man of today bears a residual pain. Then Ma Ninotte, with a sunken heart, managed the impossible. She found a stored-up penny in some emergency fund and bought two figurines. Every year, or every day, or every week, in any case in keeping with the rhythm of her wallet's fortunes, she bought Christmas figures. With her first wages as a teacher, Anastasia bought herself a pile of them. The characters, each enveloped in newspaper, were stuffed into a potato crate in anticipation of the Nativity scene. Thus every Christmas the little boy was invited to the opening of the sanctuary.

Anastasia dusted off the box with calculated slowness, her reputedly harsh eye scanning the circle that had formed around her, the smallest ones in front, the tallest behind. Paul, the musician, forgot about his guitar; Marielle abandonned her bed and her precious possessions; Jojo kept a piece of paper and a stub of a pencil with him, so as not to miss out on a formula that might unexpectedly pop out of his numerical reveries. Once the box was open, the priestess unwrapped the shapeless balls of her treasure one by one. The characters were unrecognizable in their bundles of paper. It was impossible for anyone to guess which one Anastasia was extracting from her pile. And the appearance of each character sent us into raptures; the rapture of a birth, a rebirth, echoing regularly over the years with the same heart-stopping emotion, the same happiness. There were so many of them that, after the official characters, a population of anonymous shepherds or indefinable creatures emerged for which we had to find names and create lives. Anastasia's manger was inhabited by a population the cathedral priest would have had some trouble blessing:

fat-footed philomenes,
chicken-thief-zizines,
coulirous-coolies,
Chinese-rice-people,
fried-fish-merchants,
dachine-planters,
beefy-seed-cutters
dorlis
kalazazas
hairy chabins
high-heeled she-devils
green-mango-suckers,

profiteering hedonists,
puffy manicou-headed fellows,
skinny wide-idiot-eyed pimps,
cheeky buttocks on tiny little legs,
people sickly and sore-covered,

and other groupings my mind is too timid now to describe.
And they all came there for reasons that will ultimately be lost
and that, in our blasphemous heads, probably turned into popular balls, revelry, and various and sundry bacchanalia, of which
the country has no lack of variety.

Anastasia understood the art of the manger. She bought herself
a special paper that looked like rock, which she laid, cleverly
crumpled, on one wall of the living room. In its center the
official figures were posed in the illuminated aperture, creating
a scene that never changed but was so laden with stories we spent
hours scrutinizing it. Outside, the other characters inhabited the
craggy slopes, which Anastasia covered with snow, pine trees,
rocks, stars, iridescent accessories, and blinking lights. In the
end we had the most beautiful manger in town. It was like
a dream in the house, something foreign yet close, which we
reinterpreted to give it meaning. What a mystery the snow was,
which wasn't snow anymore but cosmic festive powder, powder
of hope and happiness! How odd the pine trees were, which
were no longer pine trees but magic feet! What power these
pulsating lights possessed, which could carry you far away! The
little boy plunged into the world of the manger with unprece-
dented happiness. He never noticed that all these characters
were white, even if one of the kings seemed a little more mysterious to him than the others. What lay before him was a break in
the rational order established by the grownups, a bit of dream
made concrete, an official marvel in which he could lose himself
without feeling incomplete. The revenge Anastasia took on the

world with such determination offered him, for useful years, the perfect place to maintain the coordinates of innocence.

Prowling around outside was a Christmas of ash, blood, and fire, something incomprehensible that rose up and inflamed Fort-de-France, shattering all the magic. The police scoured the streets in pursuit of rage-filled blacks who broke into shops. The radio broadcast appeals in solemn French. We watched as the smoke of tear gas curled against facades, forcing Ma Ninotte to close her windows. Visitors whispered about news of barricades, fires, the military, and arrogant whites. The city unraveled. From its innermost depths sprouted the fruits of pain. Everyone was bewildered for two or three days. The Syrians protected themselves beneath the clanking of thirteen locks. The evening merchants (of milk, of fish, of skins) stayed away. The slatted shutters beat like dazzled eyelids. Behind them shone gazes eager to explore the world even better than a flying bat. And there was a silence—I'm talking about unusual sounds. Ma Ninotte stayed outside and protected us from them. While continuing her stocking of Christmas treats, she seemed to live as if nothing were different, except when she couldn't take it anymore and would lean out the window above the breaking bottles to scream at who knows who: "Pété fwa yo!" Destroy them! And sometimes I saw her smile at the jolting reddish glow of the suffering city. There's prowling this Christmas down below.

The new year offered new opportunities. Ma Ninotte made a point of grasping them all. None of the previous year's miseries should subsist. None of the dust, of course, but also none of the spiders or their threads, the cockroaches decimated with fly-tox. We had to change the leaves and their bark, aerate the earth from the roots up, position ourselves differently in the sun. Some went to the seashore for baths that commemorated new beginnings, others knew of virginal cascades. In the city, in tubs and under faucets, following doses of three-leafed prescriptions, we rubbed ourselves with a water green with glacial mint, white verbena, basil, or blessed charcoal. Ma Ninotte turned the house inside out. She bargained with the Syrians for linoleum for the floor. And the month of January saw the arrival of the painter with new colors — an enormous, jovial black man who possessed the subtle science of brushes and water paints. He spent a day scraping the walls, brushing them, puttying their joints, camouflaging their holes. Then, on top of the preparatory coat, he put color, ceilings always white, walls blue, walls green, walls bright yellow. As he worked, the jovial painter sang in every language of the world. He didn't know any of them, had never set foot outside the country; the only other wind that had brushed his body was that of Guyana, where he had spent a brief exile of love. But he insisted on singing in what seemed to him to be, "it's true, Señora Ninotte," the most extraordinary garden of creation, for man has a mouth as everywhere else in creation, but everywhere in creation it is used for a different music, "and that, Miss Ninotte, is the great miracle, think about it, Madame Ninotte, think about it." And since he didn't know a single word of any language, he jabbered away, imitating the particular accents picked up here and there around the country. The English blacks who cooked sugar for the whites had taught him the sounds of English. The coolies, with their votive cults, evoked the sound effects of Tamil and other sacred languages. The Syrians gave him a hint of Arabic. In the heights of Vauclin, he visited an old Congolese man who, from between his violet gums, drummed out African to a variety of beats. And while repainting their grocery stores, he hunted down the Chinese to hear the Babelish twang of their celestial empire. For the rest, he referred to his transistor, riding the waves for nights on end. The purified sky of its clamoring sounds transmitted distant tides to his curious ear. The little boy followed him from room to room, as he moved his ladder from place to place, repeating after him his squalling of strange languages, his intoxication of accents, and the joyful delirium when he would mix it all up in his excitement.

Thanks to the jovial painter, to his languages and colors, the apartment recovered a youth that Ma Ninotte accompanied with flowers. From her hidden treasures (four taciturn suitcases, always closed, stored in the back of the closet), she removed a velvet cloth and displayed it on the table during the first months. And everywhere seeds were sowed — orange seeds, mandarin seeds, these seeds, those seeds, grains of corn, lentil sprouts on wet cotton — all things that signalled to money the right place to take root for the year. For the seed has less of a past than a future; it represents promise for tomorrow, and behind each promise lies yet another promise.

The new year was the time for paying visits, for drinking punch and vermouth. The women from Lamentin filed through, and Ma Ninotte often took off in her prettiest dress toward the remainder of our family in the upper districts. Papa welcomed his buddies ("Heh heh, what t'cha got for the throat?"), the genetically thirsty, the destitute of the gullet. They called themselves rum philosophers, for they knew how to analyze its flavors even though they swallowed it straight, in one sip, without sugar, without water, without fear, with just an imperceptible straying of the pupil to accompany the pleasure of the drink as it went down. I have no memory of their conversations. The children, after their deferential greetings, were distanced from the grownups. ("Ho, the rum belongs to the bottle, my gosh.") They were never very numerous. They came, they went. Punch masses are not celebrated in large numbers; it is something between the parliament and a private assembly, a cross between explosive rackets and hushed complicity. Its protocol revolves around creating as many pretexts to drink as possible. You drink to the new arrival or to the one that's soon to arrive. You drink to the one who's leaving, the one who's about to leave, and the one who has almost left. You drink for the dead that year, and each time you laugh. The drink is preceded by a fundamental declaration on life or on Césaire. And you drink to follow what your fellow drinker is forced to repeat. And you head off to a date for punch in other places. The urban rum mass takes place between eleven thirty and one o'clock. Visitors at this hour hop from glass to glass, must be greeted, must be served. To hang around means losing out on other events; you have to drink fast and say your piece.

O Lord, preserve us from water!

Place it, measure it, lay it down, I'll set it straight!

Oh, if my mother's nipples had been filled with rum, I'd still be on all fours!

This is the assassin that killed my papa, that killed my mama, and it'll kill me!

Whoa there on the syrup; it gives cirrhosis, oh!

O rum, sole object of my desires!

Whoever felt pain was reassured: "It's the bottle that saves us, faith that kills!" And they toasted the propagation of faith among the infidels, the tears of youth, the memories of colonial wars, and especially the bottle itself, whose appearance made everyone thirsty, and vice versa, and on and on.

Booboos oozed on each knee
So many decorations of honor.

The big kids lived in a world of their own. The little boy saw himself as excluded, as if in parenthesis. His dream was to go to school like the others, to discover the city like the others, this city of which he knew only the view of his street. He, personally, possessed another world, a strangely invalidated one, the inexhaustible wealth of which made him dizzy. But he caught himself yearning for the big kid's world with a confused impatience. He was getting his first taste of a dissatisfaction he had no idea was inherent to man himself. He knew how to live in the shadows and the silence, to keep his gaze at eye level, where no one else bothered to look anymore. And he made the decision to see what he saw as he saw it, resolved to explore his inexpressible state.

In the afternoon Ma Ninotte sewed the children's clothing or made crêpe-paper flowers according to an art she had learned in her childhood, it seems, at the local sacristy, in Lamentin. Roses, gladiolas, and carnations for Mother's Day, All Saints' Day, and birthdays. She delivered them to a lady at the market, with whom she shared the profits. Sitting facing the window, in front of her sewing machine with its gentle rattling noise, she seemed to leave the world behind, didn't sing, didn't speak, didn't look, didn't see, forgot even the little boy nestled at her feet near a margarine tub transformed into a container for buttons, needles, tangled threads, and scraps of cloth for patches. Around them the house dozed to the vague sounds of dishes, the whisper of radios, the sighs of the wood, the distant poetry of another machine. The mamas never rested. They simply moved into a different type of work and a different pace. But they no longer tolerated any agitation. The little boy had to learn to take up less space, to reduce his gestures, his demands, to cram himself under a tortoise shell and adopt its economical existence. The sounds of the street grew quieter. The Syrians dozed behind their cash drawers or bandaged their wounds of exile by seeking their country in the depths of enormous radios. The afternoon slipped away like that until the return of the big

Feeling 43

kids, liberated from school, and the subsequent revving up of the city.

He had ten thousand questions. Ma Ninotte soon grew tired of answering them. "Life," she groaned, "is already broken enough without breaking it any more with broken questions." Without knowing what they were, the little boy noticed that she functioned according to a number of certainties, maybe four, five, or six, one of which was the requirement that her children succeed. She had resolved not to deviate from or question them. And especially to pay whatever price. Thus, she held misfortune by the collar, which meant misfortune had a hard time escaping her. And while the little boy divided the buttons by color, untangled a ball of wool, or tortured himself with pointless questions, Ma Ninotte retrieved a pair of shorts from perdition, prolonging its utility for a few more months. She left her machine with a step so assured that the little boy suspected her of planning her moments to come down to the second: the cook-it, the soak-it, the go-out-and-get-it, the go-see at the market. Her evenings were organized with clockwork precision that left no room for daydreaming, or mood swings—or, needless to say, for questions.

He followed her every step; he needed her presence. She tolerated him at her feet, except near the stove. He was devastated when she headed for the stairs and went out into the street, toward the merchant who sold vegetables for soup. He was afraid he'd never see her again and stood in silent horror until her return. But since she always came back, he vaguely learned to tame this fear.

Evenings were soothing: Ma Ninotte wouldn't be going out again. It was the moment for a new touch-up of the eternal soup, the moment to fry the cod, the scad, and the *coulirous* whitefish. Night ripened amid the scents of fried onions, fresh pepper, marrow exalted in vegetable soup. While cooking, she quizzed the big kids on their homework, listened to stumbling explanations, summaries of natural science, history of France, hypotenuses, and surfaces. Ma Ninotte seemed to master science better than the books themselves. In reality all she did was gauge a hesitation, the shakiness of a word, a sidelong glance beneath a tremulous eyelid. She tracked the tiniest detail until she received the firmness of a perfect recitation, the badge of true knowledge. When, years later, the little boy had to undergo the same test, he had observed her technique so often that he managed, initially, to camouflage his ignorance. But Ma Ninotte caught on. One evening, as he was floundering in a firm voice about some half-invented story of Gauls, she raised her eyes from her pots and threw back her head, silent as a cemetery. Then she explained to him, gently, yes, that you could learn monkey business, but never better than an old monkey. From then on, she had a hard time trusting him. The little boy ended up being forced to recite his lessons twice as well as everyone else and to start over at the slightest hint of a shadow of a stutter.

The dinner table was the place where accounts were settled among the older kids. Matters capable of halting creation: a missing comb, a diary whose cover had been unstapled, the dishwashing that hadn't been done, the fact that someone had tattled. Beatings were promised, live skinnings, eternal hatred was sworn, which was often extinguished with the final mouthful. Ma Ninotte calmed passions by distributing soup, fried fish, a piece of avocado, some salad. One's plate had to be emptied; no one had the right to waste anything. She sat down when we had finished. The unraveled mattresses and the opened cots filled the vital space outside the kitchen. Only Ma Ninotte and Papa had a bed that was raised up on iron legs above us. Armed with a pump, Anastasia preventively fly-toxed all-over-every-where in order to calm the passions of the tiny cockroaches who, as soon as the lights went out, gave a party in the house.

The little boy had to hurry to his cot, mouth his prayer to the Virgin Mary (under supervision), and fall asleep as quickly as possible.

The big kids stayed up whispering in the dark, laughing, telling each other of their lives in the city. The little boy listened without ever understanding a thing. It churned around sentiments: people one liked, people one hated, so-and-so who was jealous, what's-his-name who was nice, another who was a skunk. Sometimes the talk turned to a wild and very powerful emotion, triggered by very particular beings. This thing capsized the heart, but no one had a name for it yet. Schoolmasters and -mistresses (priests of science, guardians of the host of knowledge) possessed an influence that was all out of proportion. Their manners of speaking, their words, their tics, their beings as a whole far more than their teaching became beacons based on which the big kids adjusted their own attitudes. From the dining room we could hear the murmur of Ma Ninotte and Papa combined with the clattering of their forks. There was a gravity to their nighttime voices that was never present by day. It was no doubt the moment for counting up the purse, for dealing with bills and debts, for telling one's rosary of small miseries. They talked until the radio announced *The Masters of Mystery*. Then the little boy didn't hear them anymore. He often fell asleep to that distant white man's voice, so expert in knotting your stomach with tales of horror.

Snorted in seven rhythms
the lock in the nostril ripened to yellow

"I found it!" Jojo's algebraic discoveries could come at any hour. He untangled the world into little numbers and slipped them into formulas from which he himself had a hard time escaping. And when he did get out, he shouted his war cry, no matter the hour, the deepness of our sleep, the sweetness of our dreams. What's more, these discoveries were useless to us.

Ma Ninotte's paper flowers sold well, depending on the season. There was no such thing as artificial flowers at the time. She caught the petals in a metal thread that served as their stem. This stem was dressed in a green fringe soaked in glue, into which, by swirling it, she inserted leaves of another green, cut out in various patterns. Flower by flower, the bouquets grew. To the little boy they were magnificent. They piled up below the bedroom window as the afternoon progressed. The daylight falling on them bestowed a fairy-tale quality that was deceptively natural. Pending their delivery, Ma Ninotte wrapped them in a transparent paper, which crackled like crystal. Though she seemed proud of her art, no one ever saw her pose these creations on the throne of the buffet in the light of a lovely Sunday. There she placed only fragrant, natural flowers, which a country woman delivered to her. Thus, without a word, she taught the watchful little boy that a flower is mainly a scent.

Sporadically, she made sweets. It may have been connected to her mood. Sugar days were a blessing. Ma Ninotte knew how to make everything: cakes, *sikdoj*, *filibos*, twists of color that melted on your tongue, *macawon*, *lotchios câpresses*, *la-colle-pistaches*. Ladies from good families would send her orders, and she'd stand for hours by the oven in the company of the Baroness, measuring the flour, breaking the eggs, stirring it all up, whipping the whites. The little boy was on call whenever sugar entered into the picture and made it a sweet affair. He became the taster, the tester, the measurer, the licker of spoons, forks, plates, bowls, eager to serve as the beautiful yellow dough was transformed into cake. He buttered and floured the molds, collected their overflow when they were filled. He was also the oven watcher, appointed to survey the subtleties of the color, if it was coming along, if it wasn't coming along, and how it was coming along. For the *filibos*, the *sikdoj*, the caramels and so on, Ma Ninotte used a piece of marble, on which she laid the burning pupae of the candies to cool. The little boy, kept at a distance because of the risk of burns, was granted the copper pots streaked with cooked sugar—stiffened lace of benediction.

The cakes emerged from the oven more or less grilled, more or less blackened, sometimes just right when the little boy had received the grace of an intuition. Often they had to be brought around to an orthodox color with a knife. In their decoration Anastasia the Baroness claimed to be an expert—a *mapipi*. She laid them on plates, prepared her piping nozzles and her heavenly icing, and transformed the more or less massacred blackish circles into a cake adorned with silver balls, sculpted with white swirls. For major occasions she inscribed names, wishes that surpassed the comprehension of the illiterate boy. He understood only their edible quality. To write with sugar and devour the writing. This flowered his childhood beautifully: the mystery of writing and the joy of eating. When Anastasia made a mistake, she'd peel off a letter or a word for him. He wolfed them down, entrusting his taste buds with the pleasure of decoding. The assembly of cakes gave the room an unreal baptismal atmosphere. Saddened, we hoped against all hope and logic that they wouldn't be delivered to their commissioners.

Waking up at night with Ma Ninotte to help transport the communion butter bread, a clever braid of buttery dough, laid on a sheet that wouldn't fit in the home oven. The baker granted Ma Ninotte this opportunity: to take advantage of the heat of his oven for her own use as dawn broke, once he'd completed his batches of bread. Ma Ninotte brought the little boy there more than once. Oh, the nocturnal universe of bread makers! For them, Fort-de-France was just a seething shadow. The night wind came up from the sea graves, from sleeping grasses, from lands smoking with humus. When you tumbled into the bakehouse, you left behind the calm of the outside world. It seemed like a cave under siege. Everything was heaped up, harried. The baker economized on lighting. Frightening zones of shadow surrounded the work areas. Leaves of coconut trees used to embellish crusts were piled up next to bowls turning beneath a creamy dough. Everywhere you could feel the exhalation of the sometimes open oven. An unforgettable vision, that oven. So deep. So red. It threatened life with a dragon's breath. The loaves of dough, abandoned in the distance by the long pole of the baker's assistant, seemed to live a life there that was beneficial to their health and emerged in a golden renaissance. Everything was dark and hot and heavy with a smell of imprisoned flour, of coconut straw, of reddened dust, old milk, egg yolks, stale bread, fresh bread, and forgotten bread. The oven reigned with its dormant volcanic waves. The baker and his boys seemed like its servants, obscure hierodules of a sacrificial devotion peaked by night. Ma Ninotte's butter bread cooked quickly, and in the dawning day (a brightness that rises up from all over and wanders as it waits to retract into the sun's fixed eye) we carried it back toward the thick almond chocolate of our religious communions.

First Communion Chocolate
to write it is to salivate
to think of it is to suffer
to commune is chocolate

You never leave childhood, you hold it tight inside. You never detach from it, you repress it. It's not a process of improvement that leads to adulthood, but the slow sedimentation of a crust around a sensitive state that will be the core of what you are. You never leave childhood, you begin to believe in reality, what is said to be real. Reality is firm, stable, often drawn at right angles—and comfortable. What is real (which the child perceives in close proximity) is a complex, uncomfortable deflagration of possibilities and impossibilities. To grow up is to cease to have the strength to perceive it. Or else to erect a mental shield between this perception and the self. That's why poets never grow up, or so little.

"The water's here! The water's here!" Water was a daily event. Fort-de-France was just beginning to tame running water, piped in to the home. We had more or less abandoned the public fountains, epicenters of early morning riots, which still took place in the neighborhoods of the surrounding bluffs. By the time the little boy came on the scene, downtown had passed beyond that stage. On street corners the occasional flow of the decorated old fountains sometimes met with total indifference. They would dry up, then disappear, without anyone thinking to preserve their memory. The home pipe emptied into the first tub of the courtyard. There it discharged a water that ran only during certain hours. Early in the morning, at five o'clock, it spurted from the open faucet, disappeared at seven, reappearing from noon to two. For evening business we had to wait until five and move quickly because it dried up at the stroke of six. And that was the last we heard of it until morning. The little boy was present in the days when the arrival of the water still held great mystery, almost like a daily gift from the Good Lord. Each child dreamed of announcing it to the grownups, who urgently filled up pots and basins. No drop should lack for the day's necessities. As a result there was always someone who got out of bed and stood waiting near the hall window, watching the copper faucet silently as day dawned over the courtyard. The suspense sometimes lasted a while. Precision was not native to the municipal employee, and sometimes he was even late. At other hours, no, not so rare, the water gurgled sickly beneath the noon siren or, worse, didn't turn up until the next day.

Thus its arrival remained a pleasant surprise that had to be announced: "The water's here! The water's here!" The discoverer began spinning in the hallway like a drunken top off kilter, or like the Madeiran hummingbird struck by the sun in the center of its head.

"The water's here! The water's here!" And everyone ran-and-got-it, pushing and shoving, regulating the speed of the water on offer. First the grownups. Ma Ninotte, always in the lead, filled her tub, then her basins, then six or seven other containers, then some pots, then her carafes. The other mamas did the same. Each one bantered from behind:

"Well, well, Mrs. So-and-so, you don't rush your little body?"

"Oh, my God, eternity's descended on earth and she's come to visit us!"

"Ayyy! If you take your time, I'm going to take my sweet time too!"

"Hah, those donkeys don't budge, they're all the same!"

In fact, everyone stocked water well beyond what was needed for a day's use: there was always a vague fear that the city would change its mind and stop providing it. Afterward a few short minutes were left for the children to bathe. And since we couldn't form a line, we all entered helter-skelter beneath the stream. The eldest, guardians of good hygiene, ran after us for a little soaping up, a scouring of the neck, the positioning of a toothbrush. But it degenerated into a merciless war, a kind of antique water festival performed every morning, just like that of the dragonflies, whose codes the little boy already knew.

A little song for my carafe: it holds water in the shade forever, infusing the taste of an ancient well. It seals the water and becomes its accomplice, it inhabits the water and the water inhabits it, and they melt so well together that, in the worst of the heat, their heart is cool.

"The water's here" meant for the children: the party's on. The grownups approached it from the perspective of utility, with a little anxiety. You had to measure right, or you'd find yourself begging water from Mrs. So-and-so to finish some washing or, worse, drawing from the reserve of another woman who, you could plainly see, didn't need it. Each one counted her basins and her buckets, checked her tub, surveyed the height of her water like a farmer the leaves of his yams. "The water's here" meant: watch out, consider your day, and calculate everything that could go wrong.

The big water day for Ma Ninotte was Monday, the wash day. She carried the week's sheets and clothing down to the courtyard, an outlandish pile that reached to her waist. This task was confronted with song, as she had learned from the washerwomen of Lamentin. Soak, beat, wring, bleach, beat again, wring again, add some bluing, soap it up, rub it, wring it, and beat it, a tortuous process that the little boy followed wide-eyed, a process whose logic he didn't understand. And at the top of her lungs, Ma Ninotte sang the songs of Saint-Pierre, of Tino Rossi, of Edith Piaf, of Aznavour, of Luis Mariano, of Guetary, waltzes and tangos. "Marinella," "In the burning sky of Andalusia," "One May evening . . ." She knew the story of Ninon, crazy about nylon. Of Marie-Clémence, whose every affair, even the sweetest, was doomed. Of Gros-Carette who frequented the Manawa women on a dubious street of Saint-Pierre in the old days. She knew all about Régina, a real sweetheart of a dame, singled out by love. The story of the hunchback who, despite the ship's officers, knew how to keep his wife by giving her lunch money every day, at four in the morning. Sometimes, in the distance, behind the back wall, another washerwoman in the city responded with other songs, prompting Ma Ninotte to sing even louder, with even greater arrogance:

C'est par un soir de mai
que je l'ai rencontré
par un ciel plein de lune
l'amant aux lèvres brunes

Et depuis ce moment
je fus prise vraiment
une adorable flamme
s'alluma dans mon âme

The other's passion grew to sustain the rhythm. Ma Ninotte then dropped her laundry, inspired as all get-out; hands on her hips, concentrating on the reach of her voice, she entered into a truly resounding serenade.

Donne-moi les baisers enivrants
écrase-moi sur ton coeur aimant
fais couler le flot de tes caresses
dans mes veines avides d'ivresse

Nothing could stop her anymore, she forgot everything, preoccupied solely with defeating whoever'd had the nerve to challenge her by means of the unquestionable breadth of her repertory, the imperial resources of her voice, the cavernous echoes of her chest. Soon the adversary stopped. Silence. Ma Ninotte continued for some time — her throat off pitch, voiceless — before declaring her victory. And she roared to the world that she was unbeatable, for her true destiny was to have been an opera singer, but unfortunately her mother, who had no artistic sense nor any particular taste, had preferred the utility of a financial contribution and sent her to work as a cook for a lady in Fort-de-France. Thus the little boy knew why he was born in the city.

During the rest of the week, the courtyard was filled with drying laundry. Lightly colored cloths flailed in the tradewinds. The little boy moved among these mobile partitions, which divided the small yard into the good smells of bleach, of soap, of starch, and of cotton. Ma Ninotte never had enough room. She ended up running laundry lines on the roofs of the kitchens; the man of today still doesn't understand how she managed to get up there. The hanging laundry disturbed the dragonflies' habits. They could no longer find the tiny drops of holiday dew sparkling at the edge of the abyss. So they flew in circles, afraid of the liveliness of the sheets in the sweep of a wind. The little boy loved to bury his face in the clean cloth, to intoxicate himself on this particular bouquet. Or to sit boxed in by a few sheets, a world of damp whiteness that offered up a little soul at every breeze.

On sunshiny days, it all goes very fast. The cloth dries and stiffens, it steals discreet perfumes from the tradewinds and knows how to preserve them. It also reflects a little sky: it's the emotion of the bluing in all the colors. The sheets breathe in the world. With unsustainable determination, they take a firm stance and resist the winds. Ma Ninotte then sprinkles them with an ashy water, the secret of a flawless whiteness.

She then set about a long harvest, which piled up in her arms, covered her shoulders. She carried everything upstairs for folding sessions at which the little boy's presence was requested, sessions based on a particular science, which he was happy to accept as top secret, taking pleasure simply in stretching the sheets, in turning-twisting in order to fold them according to covert laws, which Ma Ninotte transmitted by command. And then too, she sang, she sang.

During the pressing, Ma Ninotte didn't sing. Wednesdays were devoted to the burning-hot and silent handling of three coal irons. She laid them on a basin of embers, wiped them with a clean rag, and at four in the morning began ironing the laundry folded by the Baroness. In the darkness, surrounded by the glowing coals of the embers, the irons from hell in her hand, she began with the school clothes of the big kids: cotton dresses for the girls, decorated with a touch of lace, khaki shorts and little sports shirts for the boys, sometimes patched in ways that were invisible to all. The next stage focused on Papa's white drill, a complicated elegance, the pleats of which had to descend in a straight line, and which Ma Ninotte hung, for a definitive drying, in the first sun that infiltrated the living room. Papa and the big kids found their clothes fresh as they emerged from their baths. They left after their hot chocolates, their coffee, and those sausage breads Ma Ninotte had made for them, during a break, at seven in the morning.

Leaning out the window, Ma Ninotte watched her children as they headed toward the rigors of school. Her lips mouthed two prayers. The little boy later learned that one was directed to a Saint Expedit, the other to Saint Judith. When his time came, he enjoyed the same protection, so much so that for years he felt them by his side during exams and competitions.

Then she went back to her ironing. The little boy, who remained alone with her, contemplated the formidable effort of the warrior negress against a pile of laundry that overflowed the table. She sweat. Steam emerged from the dampened cloth. She bore down on the thicker garments when the iron lost its heat and became less effectual. Then she grabbed another iron, nice and red, wiped it first with the clean rag and lubricated it with another soaked in candle wax. Before applying it to the skillfully arranged garment, she cleaned it once again. Ma Ninotte didn't say a word, didn't raise her head, appeared to be on a journey toward an inner bluff. Her hands folded, pleated, positioned collars and delicate zones with quasi-mechanical precision. She was solemn: ironing days were dangerous. It was possible to take in some kind of cold or sudden congestion. Here's why.

The world in those days was divided into hot and cold. Health lay in the balance above them. Sickness resulted when into your heat you introduced the cold of a banana or some coconut water; when the heat of your head was caught in the glacial stream of a raindrop; when on the heat of your stomach, buttons undone, you allowed to pause the sudden coolness of a wind flowing down from the heights. A mango could become a poison, for it emerged from a principle of cold that (after running an errand, at the end of the heat of an active day) could kill you on the spot (which the Creole language designates by *lan mô fwèt*—cold death, or death in cold).

If the life of the country was naturally hot, the worst was the heat of ironing. You disassembled the delicate mechanism. To stay alive afterward, you had to be careful in thirteen ways. Ma Ninotte ironed with the windows shut and the door closed. Once the work was finished, she didn't change her clothes. She wiped her sweat with a napkin the temperature of the ironing room, and for the rest of the day, she didn't touch water, stayed out of the rain and the wind, and avoided fruits with cold centers. That meant staying in the heat. The little boy, curious about this fearsome division of the world, conscientiously perspired with her.

Sometimes, just to check, he broke the balance, stood in the rain or exposed his throat to a descending wind. In the evening, a hamg-hamg cough troubled his sleep. Ma Ninotte then put her old war against sickness into gear. She herself was never sick or, if ever she was, no one saw her resting. Moreover, she rejected pharmaceutical medications, which she nonetheless gave to her children. When it came to her own body, only vegetable medications were allowed right of passage (teas, infusions, liqueurs), prescribed by the healer-merchants at the market. She knew what doses of herbs were right for her, explains the Prime Confidante, examining this contradiction. "I knew how to measure my fevers and where the pain was; my intestines, my stomach, and my heart were familiar with Guinea grass, the flavors of the good-for-everything herbs, and the cha-cha herbs. But since I didn't know the new bodies of you children, I had to let the doctor man with his medicine do his work. Because each healing plant is a kind of poison, and it's not poison the same way for everyone. I saw the cha-cha herb ruin the liver of one person in two days and do nothing to another man for over a week, except maybe make him stronger."

Thus Creole medicine was losing its paths of transmission. The man of today knows that there are now broken peoples who have to be retaught the elementary principles of medicine and hygiene, who are out of touch with their own genius, and whom others try to "develop" to the rhythm of another genius. A people becomes feeble and dies when its traditions are invalidated even to itself, when it freezes them, grasps at them, perceives them as archaic without ever adapting them to the changing times, without absorbing them and moving into modernity, armed with their wealth. So it is for us in places.

The medicine man was an old mulatto doctor, whom the little boy had to call Tonton—Uncle. He never seemed to leave his office, or his white smock, or his stethoscope. He was bald, with bushy hair around the ear, slightly crude in words but frank in manner, and as generous as the crab in the fairy tale that offers its own head. Ma Ninotte's five children (each one testing for him- or herself the order of hot and cold) forced her to consult him beyond the possibilities of her purse. Tonton didn't ask her for a penny and was always available; morning, noon, and night, Sundays and at two in the morning, he answered her calls and always found time for a visit to the sufferer of the day. When some money cropped up in the house, Ma Ninotte didn't forget him, and a ham of the Christmas pig had his name on it.

After him came the pharmacist, a slightly grumpy, taciturn giant, whose smile had faded. The little boy went to see him on command, clinging to the counter to clamor: Mama said to tell you I'm going hamg hamg hamg." Hearing this password, the man with the cement face (who never mentioned to Ma Ninotte that there were prices on the medicines) handed him a bottle of syrup, a tablet, or the oddities that Tonton had prescribed in a scribbled hand. He too unfailingly received his piece of the pig.

To be sick was to enter a realm of sweetness. Ma Ninotte became more attentive, more present, neglecting the others a little. The little boy wallowed in it shamelessly. His lack of control over his temperature was a source of deep sorrow. So on top of his coughs, his vomiting, and his asthma, he enacted extraordinary melodramas. Ma Ninotte doted on him with treats, picture books, a sweet from the market. She worried about him as soon as he came inside, tucked him in as night approached. The Baroness was attentive as well. Marielle, Paul, and Jojo, after a touch of commiseration, didn't care. To them, an illness meant one more task on the list of their domestic bothers.

The little boy was so content to be sick that Ma Ninotte had to tetanize him with a Creole word after a few days. To show him that the game was over, that he had to get vertical again, because the house was neither a hospice nor an asylum: "That child thinks life is a *bol-toloman*, oh, my Good, Good Lord, what's next, huh?"

The tin hood
brim of the facade
transformed the rain into long fragile
strings

58 *Feeling*

When it came to health, there was hot and cold, but there were also bad niggers. These people-with-powers wandered the city, jealous, envious, mean, reaping with terrifying pleasure the fruits of their evil. You had to watch out for them. The mamas were on the alert. The children were never to shout either a family name or a first name, so that no incensed wind would record them. Those evil ears plugged into the tradewinds could only be entrusted with silly and soulless nicknames. It was especially important to watch that no hand pass over one's head: children had been known to become mysteriously dimwitted. One black woman from the upper bluffs, passing by at the request of an envious neighbor, traced a finger over some kids' foreheads, and they ended up bahbah and slobbering, with big fat heads and fat knees. It was also a time when certain fishermen, having sworn allegiance to the devil, used children's flesh for their bow nets and *zins*. Others needed it to baptize some she-devil and for ceremonies that sent convoys from hell hurtling to the center of town. In addition they knew how to steal your health, yes, pick it the way you pick a mango, and place it to ripen in their sacks forever. Their victims remained yellow, in the state of those male papaw trees, unequipped for anything, even to make promises.

Against these curses Ma Ninotte had weapons distributed throughout the house, in her laundry, in her wallet, in front of her door, on window ledges. Upon the birth of each of her children, she had done what was necessary so that no harm doer should sink his hooks into them (for their intelligence as well, she had worked according to tradition, with honey, herbs, and oils, in dosages that, to her mind, had been just right for the number cruncher, but a wee bit off for the lymphatic and over-sensitive little boy). But the declaration of an illness elicited the following calculation: is it a hot-cold problem or an attack by a bad nigger? Such that even before going to see Tonton, and at least twice a year, and even without any illness, the little boy received a bath in guardian leaves—from geraniums, poppies, patchouli, and silk-cotton trees—that softened his skin, fought against dartres or other funguses, and at the same time unclogged from his pores any possible evil spells.

The little boy plunged into his magic baths feverish in spirit. He emerged the bearer of an invisible armor, immortal and powerful. Without further ado, he headed for the bottom of the stairs or the kitchen roofs to confront, unbeknownst to everyone and with his eyes closed, a seven-headed monster with yellow teeth who lived in the attic of his nocturnal fears.

After the bad niggers, another possibility was raised: worms. Creole sickness can also come from worms. Ma Ninotte (like all the mamas) watched for their evildoings in the slightest disturbance of her children—in the eye, on the nail, in the elasticity of the belly, in this, in that. The little boy had to undergo frequent purges against worms (even though he never saw any emerging from his body) and imbibe copious infusions steeped in a sickly herb that came up at certain times straight above the masonry walls and that Ma Ninotte said was bad to the smell, good in its effect, and saintly in its principle.

Otherwise you had to fall back on hot and cold and restore the balance with the help of Tonton and the pharmacist.

At the window
after a teardrop
daydream of the city and sleep with it

Beneath the beds Ma Ninotte sometimes let rabbits loose, which circulated in the house until their fatal Sunday. The albino rabbits were the most striking: beautiful, with pink eyes, but as vicious as they come. They haunted the underside of the furniture like zombis on Holy Week, materializing in the kitchen for a piece of carrot, burrowing the rest of the time among the dying shoes that were crammed beneath the beds. That's because Ma Ninotte threw nothing away. Old underwear resided under the mattress, becoming stuffers useful for clowning around or for patches. Sometimes it was called back into service for the unimaginably needy whom Ma Ninotte visited behind the gullies. During big cleanups we puffed up the mattresses and their linen. Each of us then found him- or herself amid what had become the archeological strata of the family: ancient panties, ageless boxers, a minuscule nightshirt that reduced the imperial posturing of the Baroness a notch (despite her fancy airs, she had fit into that!). The dead shoes stayed there, in the hope of a hypothetical moment of leisure during which Papa (a former shoemaker, yes, but one who had kept his tools despite his new job as a postman) could take up the implements of his art and transform the thick, shapeless old shoes into shiny loafers or, at the very least, into school shoes. Sometimes he had to perform his miracle, but most of the time (since the Syrians brought back marvels from Italy, which held up well, didn't need to be softened with rum, and adapted to the foot without causing suffering) these shoes served as a funerary landscape for the rabbits whose ferocity was white, and each beady pupil pink.

Remember: the Eleventh-Hour Knight blossoms at eleven, is good for the liver and wounds, and looks like a thick grass.

Shut in since the death of his best friend, the pharmacist, they say, no longer drinks, no longer eats. He lives on memories and feeds on daydreams. You have to imagine him among his strange bottles, the color of bandages, full of hieratic powders, which he dispensed behind the counter. He looked like a moth, emptying his shelves for the poor women who asked. His pharmacy smelled mostly of ether, and perhaps aspirin. It straddled two worlds: his shelves bore witness to another very ancient pharmacopeia that he must have practiced in his pharmacist youth and whose vestiges he had relegated, unwillingly, to dusty heights no longer touched. As for Tonton, the Prime Confidante claims to see him still, immobilized in an old age that no longer matures. He lives and conducts himself as if he had never been a doctor; he's simply gone on to something else, like one who doubts the values of this earth and who sails to the winds of curiosity, with the dazzled gaze of shipwrecked sailors toward a lighthouse. Neither one practices anymore. They live in slow motion somewhere, among children and grandchildren who may not even know the heights of their devotion. I see them as immortal, as everlasting as certain trees. It is from them that the man of today gets his inclination toward open hands and his inability to say no to what is asked of him. He knows — happily, out of weakness — how to give.

"Now this one, when full of the juice of the grape one day, and down at the bottom of a bottle all his wits lay . . ." There's the image of Papa-the-shoemaker. It's hazy. Who's talking memory? What prowler remembers? He's seated near the window, the small anvil on his knee, hammering the heel of a shoe, cutting the leather with the paring knife, stitching with the awl, filing, tinting, brushing, waxing, and shining. Around him the shoes to be repaired pile up, deformed and ragged. And he, to the little boy who's watching him, trills his impeccable French, molds his ceremonial voice into careful expressions and the shapes of his thoughts. He knows the power of the French language and at times counters Ma Ninotte's ire with a touch of Corneille, a decree of La Bruyère. His favorite is La Fontaine, of whom he recites entire fables to the little boy, and while he doesn't know them all, he knows all their morals. "Now this one, when full of the juice of the grape one day, and down at the bottom of a bottle all his wits lay, his wife installed him inside a certain tomb . . ." To recite, he half shut his lids around a joyful vision, his lips alive with reverential malice, and lifted the tool in his hand, emphasizing the curve of each word. He savors the work performed on verse, knows how to convey the music and carve out silences, to slide quickly over a hump in the syllables. His smile illuminates the cadence and an exclamatory chuckle racks his body crouched over the anvil: "Is there nothing to drink in this tomb?"

The shoemaker would later abandon his tools for the job of postman in Fort-de-France. He traveled the borderlands of Pichevin Bluff, the heights of the Route des Religieuses, and the Coridon Quarters. The little boy watched him appear at punch time or in the evening, exhibit his uniform with its fat gold buttons, and reemerge spick-and-span as an official in his white cotton drill. Later the little boy would find classical records that Papa had savored on his gramophone in the days of his youth. They say he even played a pretty good fiddle in some mutual-aid society, catapulting the ladies into hyperventilated dizzy spells. They say too that he held lengthy conversations with the president of this society on the sharpness of a language that the Baroness honed with him. The little boy knew him only as a mulatto with a white mane, sententious and domineering, erecting the cathedrals of a high French in the course of his punch gatherings. Or else very gentle, attentive, kind, dispensing nicknames and an occasional tender pat on the head to those he loved. Or else absent and sad, indifferent, sipping bitter punch in the company of an even more somber friend. Or else, later, at his retirement window, on the lookout for the still active colleague descending the street, sack on his hip, letter in his teeth, and signaling to him with a pale, elderly hand. To the little boy he recited La Fontaine, and the fool is hungry for more. Oh memory, is there mink oil in the beatings of the heart?

Everyone's hair was different. Paul's and Marielle's was blue-black and less frizzy, a little like the Indian coolies'. Anastasia had the thick locks of a *câpresse*: it covered her shoulder blades, and no one knew what to do with it. Jojo and the little boy lifted it into little zeros plus zero plus zero. Papa deployed a mulatto's bouquet, dense and swelling. Ma Ninotte disciplined her negress hair beneath a madras kerchief. Among the hallway crowd, the spectrum was even wider. What wasn't frizzy was called nice-hair or coolie-hair or beautiful-hair. The rest was on the order of straw, iron, steel wool, a helmet, prickly grass, or rubble—names that signified something quite unenviable. Nice hair accepted the comb, a little comb made of bone with epileptically tight teeth, with which one obstinately attempted to dominate hairdos in the here-below. And gradually, gradually, this embittered comb for string-hair resigned, abandoning its teeth one by one on the heads of the damned. Marielle and Paul could vaguely use it, but the others were subjected to its thirteen hells. And without ever thinking to curse the wretched comb, they cursed their own hair.

Among the little boy's crowd, hours were spent brushing the frizziness. The mamas liked to have it shorn off at the shop of the lame barber, a kind of fallen athlete, wielding his shaver, cologne water, and a razor, who seemed to hate any black hair that wasn't drowning in the scalp. And on these shaved heads he smoothed a softening vaseline, then planed it down with a triumphant brush. On the staircase, after the massacre, we compared the specks of our hair, accompanying its regrowth with hours of smoothing, so much so that—stretched out, flabby, exhausted by our obstination—it began to wave, to die almost, in order to resemble hair.

Oh, the days of vaseline and brushes! The women tackled the defrizzing iron, and on Sunday afternoons the city dozed to the smells of stewed pomade and fried locks.

Along with dandruff, bad hair was an illness that could be transmitted through the comb. Thus a comb was never lent—much less a brush. For those who had the choice not to share it was *my* comb and *my* things. To touch them was like signing a warrant for one's death. It was the only way to avoid an epidemic in the same family, or to spare the family from being infected by our stricken country.

And yet Anastasia the Baroness possessed the most beautiful hair in the world, something luxurious, generous, which covered her scalp like a growth of soft ivy. Ma Ninotte spent Sunday afternoons untangling it into little plaits, brushing it, wrapping it in curl paper. The Baroness played the martyr and abandoned her pride. We watched her, lips tight, silent, breathe ah, ah, ah without eating peppers and perspire without climbing the slightest hill. "What am I going to do with this hair, what am I going to do with this hair?" Ma Ninotte would sigh as she went off in search of her horn comb.

O my Baroness, you had the most beautiful hair in the world. Often the little boy saw her, on the occasion of mysterious balls, dressed in the style of the French Middle Ages. Several of us would lace her into an asphyxiating corset. The swellings of a hoop skirt gave her the hips of a mother duchess on the Pont d'Avignon. And on top of this surreal garment—a striking touch—she unfurled her *câpresse* hair in undulating, twisting waves, a hair dizzying in abundance, with a hint of tawny *chabine* reflections, a hair that didn't play in the wind but played with the wind, that sat on her shoulder with a vaporous and massive stiffness that nothing seemed able to eclipse. Oh, the most beautiful hair in the world—and we didn't know it.

The radio announced a cyclone. But Ma Ninotte had been informed in advance. She knew the connection between the clouds and the rats' activity. She knew how to decode the movement of small insects cast into daylight by the menacing sky. It seemed like a day of rain, but one that would be of millennial darkness, a day confusedly perceived. No one explained anything to the little boy. Everyone moved into action around him, no longer answering his questions. Ma Ninotte went looking for water containers. She stored them everywhere, filled to asphyxiation. She bought candles and matches. Refilled her reserve of kerosene and wicks. Stocked up on bread, salt, oil, dried cod, and dried beans. Brought home a salted slab of meat. Checked her tincture of arnica, her ether, her supply of camphorated rum and of leaves for dressing wounds. She removed her most precious objects from the courtyard and carried them up to the hallway. In the house, the emergency plans against seepages were reinforced; she checked the tightness of the windows, whose creaking wood always required a little filing. The shutters were closed shut with tiny nails. In the meantime, the light had faded. The little boy never saw a daytime cyclone. Always at night, as if to give the world time to submit, for the Syrians to close their shops, for the streets to empty out, for those who possessed automobiles to park them tightly on the upper bluffs. Then, in a sickly silence, in the rain and the first winds, we began to wait, to wait, to wait, to take the waiting and store it.

The little boy didn't know quite what everyone was waiting for. The word "cyclone" meant zip to him. He didn't understand the immobility on people's faces, the truce in the usual wars, the skimping on gossip at the evening meals, the difficulty sleeping. One's slightest words were greeted with "Sleep" or "Quiet over there." Ma Ninotte came-and-went, checked what she had already checked, paused next to the radio to find out what-was-happening. Papa camped in front, his ear to the music, and gave the alert when the voice of the announcer suspended the broadcast. We waited. For his first cyclone the little boy got sleepy too soon and, naturally, no one woke him.

When he did awaken he understood what they'd been waiting for. The city lay defeated, covered with mud, floods, and strange objects. Tin sheets were scattered throughout the streets, fallen trees lifted nightmarish roots in a flow of black water, white pigs and featherless chickens and hornless oxen searched, stunned, for a steady order to the world. The smashed-in store-fronts released a vomiting of floods. Fat electrical wires jumped at the discharge of their own sparks. Lying everywhere were orphaned cupboards, big broken mirrors, a floating safe, a thousand drawers without pasts, enormous books swelled with water, the bric-a-brac of a jumbled Caribbean hamper, an absolute sacking, racking, higgledy-piggledy of pockets of the sky, of hearts and attics. Above it all, the shrieking dismay of the first arrivals discovering what the old-folks call (or more exactly cry) "an tÿou-manman"; what Césaire would call "a disaster."

Cyclones are colorblind. They overturn the possessions of whites and mulattos, they skin life and, for several days, redistribute the parts. In the city the world started over beneath a sea of mud way up to there. The people of the seven bluffs, who were generally spared, came running to try their luck in the gutted stores. Without thinking, the Syrians began selling off their mud-laden rolls of cloth as earthen bricks. Police, firemen, politicians, solemn madmen, sack-carrying negresses, desperate day workers, *chabins* on all fours: a virtual hill of frantic ants busy with survival, yet attentive to the wink of a blessing.

The little boy spent days at the window, following Ma Ninotte through the neighborhood with his eyes. Never was she more at ease than in the apocalypse. If there was no more water, she brought water. If there was no more fish, she hauled in fish. She found hot bread. She found candles. She found packages of dreams and carted them, balanced atop her big hat. And, especially, she brought back mud-drenched clothing by the armful, snippets of cloth wrested from a black cement, lost objects covered with a nameless gangue. They mounted up in the courtyard in anticipation of a cleaning. He watched her disappear down one street and reappear via another, massive and powerful beneath the wings of her hat, talking loud, greeting everyone, distributing unsolicited advice. For this adversary of ill fortune, disaster was an old friend. She was hardly more active than usual and managed to extract the best for us. Yet she never received news of an impending cyclone greedily, like a sick man presented with chicken soup. She would have gladly done without it. Once a cyclone had passed, however, she launched into battle as if she had been the strategist and, beneath each misfortune, unearthed each piece of luck. In these times the tilt of nature leaned to the side of the have-nots.

Someone had to worry about the villages. Information arrived in snatches: such-and-such a place cut off from God, this cross under water, that town toppled to the bottom of a cliff. As soon as the roads were reestablished, Ma Ninotte went off in person for word of the family. Otherwise she kept an ear out for news of funerals and attended the burials of those whose hearts couldn't take the ventilation, who had drowned to save their pigs, been cut in half by a flying piece of tin, or swept off in the suicide of an enraged water toward the sea.

We lost an uncle. He sailed beyond the sky with his favorite kid goat. His concubine saw him rise with the wind, the kid under his arm, barely a look of surprise on his face to find himself in a sea unfurling its waves above the tall trees. We never saw him again, except during certain storms, when the merchants of coal filled the sky and it began to rain not just water but nights of old. His concubine and children heard him announcing destinies to come, express concern about their health and the other goats. He also mentioned quite often his fighting cock, which no one dared take into combat anymore and which was wasting away like an old hen at the foot of a silk-cotton tree. Ma Ninotte, when she went up, tried to talk to him, but all she got in response was a bleating over gurgles of wind. From then on, no one understood him anymore.

A medium was brought in, a zombi-talker, one of those Negroes who straddle day and night. The fellow approached the house sleeping during one of those rains with a name. In his sleep, he began to speak to uncle. He spoke to him in a distant Creole, in an old French, in a collection of languages that have hung around the Caribbean since a time when the world was simple. And uncle answered him with the bleating of a kid and underground wind. When he awoke, the medium announced that he hadn't understood this celestial gibberish and that nothing could be drawn from it—because it's true, madam, that when carried off by a cyclone you find yourself twirling in your brain somewhere that's never clear, to say the least. Our uncle would wander like that for three-quarters of eternity plus a number of hours equal to that of the hairs on the kid to which his soul was henceforth joined, he confided in them as he fled.

The mud encrusted the city for months. The street sweepers took away the majority of it, the firemen chased the rest away with jets of water. Yet there subsisted an invincible film that only daily life could hope to dissolve. For the little boy this was a strange phenomenon: a wind comes and floods, a breeze passes and breaks into black mud. A city dies to emerge new from a filthy mummification. Abundance sprouts from misfortune: in the sticky streets we found seventy-two illusions and other dreams that no longer flew.

The postcyclone brought the children together. The school was flooded. Sleeping late was allowed. The grownups, busy with cleaning, granted them a bit of inattention. The home troop filled the hallway with its games. Then sometimes Jeanne-Yvette got into the act. She came from somewhere unknown and boarded with Ma Sirène's family on occasion. A thin girl, yes, laughing, ferocious, lovable, and gentle to boot. She brought us Creole tales from the country unknown in our Fort-de-France nights. City storytellers were rare. In any event, the little boy had never seen one. He encountered the Creole folktale with Jeanne-Yvette, a real storyteller, which is to say, unfathomable in memory and unbeatably cruel. She scared you to death with two words, a hint, a meaningless song. She played on silence, on language. She splattered death with laughter, gathering this laughter from terror alone. She led us along to the rhythm of her tongue's squalls, making us believe anything. We watched for Mama Dlo in the shadow of the stairs. We ran-for-it at the smell of a zombi she sniffed. She forced us to undress at the mention of a she-devil who hated clothing. She taught the little boy the astonishing richness of Creole orality. A universe of canny resistance, of salvational cruelty, rich with several genies. Jeanne-Yvette came to us from Caribbean memories, from the swarming of Africa, from the diversities of Europe, from the festering of India, from the quakes of Asia, from the vast touch of the peoples in the prism of the open islands, the very sites of Creolity.

Her favorite character was Mama Dlo, a water divinity who forced respect for the rivers or the sea. She kidnapped adventurous children near waterfalls unbeknownst to their parents. Jeanne-Yvette spoke of her without describing her. She focused on an indefinable head of hair ever smoothed by a beautiful comb, on gestures suffused with grace. To see Mama Dlo was to fall under the spell of the push-pull charm of a heartless creature. She drew you in only to perform cruelties to which Jeanne-Yvette taught the answer. *O wise woman!* She knew what to do to ward off Madame Banse's ever so despicable children, how to react to the limping of the three-hoofed horse, to the evil hand of a coffin a tad too friendly, to the trailing shadow of a silk-cotton tree. She knew the virtue of salt when the skin of an "engagé"—a man who'd made a pact with a spiritual power—shone on the branches of a docile acacia. She showed us the orange that was safe for calming she-devils and the movement that gives away toads that are not what they seem. She revealed to us the victories of ruse, of vice, of patience, and of the brainchild that hit just at the right moment. There was no point speaking full throttle, she would say in secret; better to whisper. Two fingers often equalled an entire fist. Going straight was not the best means to arrive at a place, and if the paths turned circles in the woods, often you had to turn with them: those who followed the straight roads, which the white mill owners had paved for themselves throughout the country, were lost. To travel them was to serve those people. You had to follow the paths, scribble their order of Maroon madness. With her opaque method, Jeanne-Yvette taught us about life. She gave the little boy a sense of the impenetrable strategy of strength of Ma Ninotte, in fact, and of the other mamas of the city.

A certain one of us lived at the other end of the hall. It was hard for him to leave the storytelling circle and go home: he would have had to confront a shadow that Jeanne-Yvette had laced with terror. In her cruelty, everything always ended badly: some *soucougnan*, she revealed, was crouched at the top of the stairs; he had followed her to gauge her lies and her respect for rituals; she felt his musk of bitter guava oozing from the thirteenth step. Jeanne-Yvette knew how to wipe him out with a single Creole cry, so she wasn't afraid, but woe betide those who didn't know that word. The hall-crossers begged for this word that would allow them to remain alive. "You have to learn," exclaimed Jeanne-Yvette in triumph, "how to live with life, you city brats, who know nothing of the world! Come learn with me in the country, you dimwits." The hall-crosser then had to fly, wings aflutter, across the ten yards of hallway transformed into an abyss.

Leaving

Noon siren: Ma Ninotte stops and sits. Papa shows up. A thirsty visitor arrives. The little boy has to dash over to the Chérinote bar to ask for a piece of ice, a bottle of Didier water. Other times he has to run to the grocery store and bring back a *musse* of rum. The city slows down a pace. In the streets only the overexcited persist, or the adversaries of a misfortune that forbids lifting a foot. It's the punch hour: when the little boy runs, he has no shadow.

The green mango
tortured to a luscious cream
of its pigeon-caca
if the feast is sacred so is the mango
not to mention the season

He's happy because he's starting to get out into the city. He had observed it from windows. For him, Fort-de-France was the Syrian street, an interminable street bordered by the sea at one end and the Place de la Croix-Mission at the other. It was the most congested and best stocked, an unavoidable central axis. The vegetable market flanked its center; the fish market hung like a bell from one of its ends. The slaughterhouse wasn't far, nor the white men's warehouses where the small-town grocers stocked up on supplies. Everything passed through there, and there lay the city.

The little boy knew its every rhythm. At dawn, its creamy sun, its coco-heart light, its sad dogs of the night beneath the prison of the day. Distracted by endless emergencies, two or three madmen tread and retread barely a yard. The white truck delivered its blocks of ice. The Syrians dominated the commerce of cloth, shoes, pots, and oilcloths. Arriving good and early, standing on a street corner, they exchanged words on questions of war in the Middle East and lifted their metal curtains when their salesgirls appeared. The sound of the curtains rising is the first song of the city, hesitant at first, then continuous, and finally harsh as a retracted spring. This brought sound effects to the street at different hours, according to whether the Syrian had opened completely or not. Because before anything else, the salesgirls set about tidying the doorstep: an unchanging ritual with bleach, disinfectant, brushes, and splashing water. The little boy had trouble understanding this ceremony: the Syrians had either cemented, tiled, or painted the stretch of sidewalk in front of their stores, and their entrances—compared to the crumbled remains of cement and mud found elsewhere—seemed perpetually bright. Yet, they scoured them at length. The little boy found this Creole ritual repeated at the vegetable market, and he realized that beyond the desire for cleanliness lay the concern to uproot any possible curse planted at night by an evil black.

The beauty of dawn: the scent of bleach, of disinfectant, of dampened sidewalks, empty streets, light, silence growing fainter with the mounting of life. It's not a city yet, just a neighborhood, our neighborhood. The locals are on the street, watering the flowers on their balconies, saying hello, exchanging chitchat. Ma Ninotte, rising before the cock, is already at work, visiting the Syrians, telling jokes to her salesgirl friends. She takes advantage of this special moment to bargain or obtain a blouse she needs, a useful cloth, or a dream remnant. Every day she brings home two or three yards of fabric of various qualities, which she sews on Sundays and every afternoon. She uses her machine to create the styles selected by the Baroness from fashion magazines. The latter too, quickly initiated into sewing, works her cloth to enter the realm of elegance, causing Marielle—who never deigned touch a needle—to drool.

> *The capsule*
> *flattened*
> *elongated*
> *sounded the thread and cut sharp*
> *thumb sliced open*
> *fingers bandaged*
> *yoyo-season of beautiful battles*

The little boy follows Ma Ninotte from afar. She doesn't even suspect it. He follows with a panicked eye. He watches her come and go, disappear into a store, exit a store, play queen of the street. People call to her, wanting to see her. They're hoping for some fish from her friends the fishermen. They sigh at the sight of the seasonal vegetables, which she alone knows how to obtain at rock-bottom prices. Back and forth, she comes and goes. The street is emerging from its dream state. The pushcarts from the villages are beginning to bottleneck at the approaches to the markets. The jobbers with their handcarts are hailing customers with baskets of fresh vegetables exuding the sugary or acidic vapors of the earth. Thirty-two merchant ladies are galloping, titties bouncing as if beating a church bell; they're afraid of a delay that might cost them a good spot. The high-school kids are walking up the street, the junior-high schoolers heading down. A mailman distributes love and pain. The bureaucrats are on the loose. Suddenly the street is stifling, noisy, dusty. People are honking, shouting, screaming, laughing. The country people talk loud and walk in the middle of the road, thinking it's still a mud path. The drivers have to beg, or threaten, them to pass.

The little boy watched the hazy tide from above. He allowed himself to be imprisoned by its odors, its sounds, its reds, yellows, and greens. Other times, he picked a woman with a basket and followed her journey from the top of the street, her hesitations and crossovers, her entries into particular stores. A Syrian would pounce on her, sweet words on his lips. He'd tap her shoulder, cover her chest with a cloth only to exclaim at how it brightened her face. He'd stick to her like a predator to its prey until she produced some change and acquired something, anything at all. The little boy felt as if he were reliving his spider-watching days.

Entering the Syrians' shops was dangerous at that time. They spoke several languages, Creole for familiarity, French to strike deals, their native tongue to simulate idiocy when the client had spunk. They knew how country people functioned, the colors they liked, their desire to participate in the age of nylon and polyester, their weakness for gold trim, their love of lace and tablecloths, their soft spot for Millet's *Angelus*. . . . Stationed in front of their boutiques, they hooked them one by one with the latest marvels. All the salesgirls did was deliver. They knew nothing about business. They presented a stony court-reporter face to every customer, didn't care whether they came inside or went away, and greeted them solely with a bored, squeaky "What t'cha want?" A Syrian who wasn't present at his store lost the day. He had to remain on watch himself, lay the bait himself, reel in the catch himself, and stab it with the price himself.

When the day was going badly, the little boy watched the Syrians change strategies, bring fabrics of a certain color to the front, stack eye-catching saucepans right in the middle of the sidewalk, unravel the nylon, wave it ecstatically, quaveringly bleat, "The latest in Paris, the latest in Paris . . . ," and boom! the neglected store was swarming, like a booboo with little flies. Clients attracted other clients, a mob formed, receded, formed again farther down the street to the devilish rhythm of Syrian pranks.

Toward midmorning the Syrians stopped to nibble a boiled onion or a spicy cod sandwich. The closest ones gathered on their common sidewalk, chatting by their stores; their eyes fixed on the waves of country people, they sought amid the credulous packs those whose faces were illuminated by a slightly thicker wallet.

Letchi
was a varnished pipe
of incomparable luster
its rare season carried cotton to drink
to old men without much age

Sometimes the Syrians were confronted by a cunning customer. He'd look like a numbskull straggling in from some distant forest. He'd put on a mask of idiocy and, in this opened bow net, the Syrian found himself trapped like a spot of redfish when the moon is askew. Here's how.

The good fellow let the Syrian talk, let him go into raptures, flatter, marvel. He seemed to have a thousand years at his disposal, went to look wherever they wanted, examined what they showed him, drooled when drooling was required. The delighted Syrian spent a lot of time with him. Then, suddenly, he acted as if he were going to leave without buying anything. The Syrian (horrified at having wasted an hour) began sweating, ready to sell anything and at any price. But the other, now closed up like a clam, seemed to need nothing and drifted toward the door. Just as he was about to leave, he changed his mind; out of the goodness of his heart, almost as a favor, he bargained for a particular product, and it was rare that the Syrian resisted for long. His purchase concluded, the cunning fellow took off without even smiling at his victory and entered, dazed, into another store. His next victim, seeing him with a package in hand, imagined his pockets to be full and launched into an enthusiastic welcome, which our man bore stoically, more placid and docile than a coconut in the rain.

With Ma Ninotte, the Syrians never bargained. They offered her a good price or gave her what she wanted. They generally had good hearts, but she forced them into it too: so energetic, so strong, so useful for so many things. They were fascinated that she knew so many people. The Syrians were very attentive to Creole customs. They observed the local people the way one observes the enigma of a tropical fruit out of season. They wanted to understand us, and they did a good job of it. Getting close to Ma Ninotte was part of a strategy of local conquest they never did complete: their children, who became Creoles, like us, with the same values, swore off the racks and shelves to study medicine, letters, or law. Those who went into the family business had gotten stuck somewhere in life and entered into the trade the way some people continue to live with their mothers. Little by little, the Syrians lost their power.

With mounting anxiety, the little boy must have followed Ma Ninotte more than once, dashing down the stairs and into the street without her noticing, tracking her from a few yards away, hidden behind people or open shutters. The Prime Confidante claims that her merchants alerted her more than once to the presence of a worried little shadow that didn't let her out of his sight, flowed in her wake, stopped when she stopped. The first time she must have gone to him, scolding, concerned he would get lost; then, other times, she must have done so laughing. Soon he could join her at the market, in her battle for fish at the bottom of the canal, at the grocery counter for rum, oil, salt, and pepper.

The mandarin
offers the weapon of its peel
eyelids watch out

eyes running the enemy cries
and the mean fingers are drowned in perfume

Ma Ninotte knew the market. Better than anyone, she knew its laws. The little boy at her heels watched her operate: approach the merchant ladies, catch up on the news, evaluate the products, and, most of all, bargain. She didn't say, "How much is this?" like tourists or city folks, but got into feelings first. She asked the merchant what was new. The latter, sensing where it was going, hurriedly knit a wary brow. But Ma Ninotte was warm, expressed concern about her children, her man, her benefits, about this and that, and interrupted this approach by finding her looking mighty fine these days. Suddenly she uncovered her basket. She went into raptures over everything, then, imperceptibly, drew in her net. The tomatoes (which didn't interest her) were beautiful-beautiful-beautiful; she came up with seven fine words to describe them. The merchant added to her praise and, already ensnared, gave her prices (usually outrageous). Ma Ninotte sighed at how much she'd like to eat them ("oh la la, your *dachines* don't look too good today") but her health wouldn't allow it, something about dizzy spells, and they're so expensive anyway, but they deserve to be expensive. During the praise of the tomatoes, she chose among the allegedly bad *dachines*, a sheer marvel, then slowly made her move:

MA NINOTTE
Someone told me stuffed tomatoes are to die for this year. . . .

THE MERCHANT
Someone told me that too.
If you want a pound, I can give you such and such a price. . . .

MA NINOTTE
Really, huh?

THE MERCHANT

Yes, really . . .

MA NINOTTE

Would I have the time to cook that today?

THE MERCHANT

So long as we're not dead, there's time. . . .

MA NINOTTE

It's too bad, gosh. . . .
Your *dachines* didn't turn out well. . . .

THE MERCHANT

Take a pound of the tomatoes, sweetie. . . .

MA NINOTTE

Will you have them tomorrow?
If you're here tomorrow, I'll take two pounds. . . .

THE MERCHANT

Tomorrow's another country. . . .

MA NINOTTE

Ah la la, the *dachines* aren't in season this year, they're not very
tempting. . . .

THE MERCHANT

What about the tomatoes?

MA NINOTTE

I told you, tomorrow, God willing.
Since you're a darling, I'll buy something today though. . . .
I know how tough life is. . . .

THE MERCHANT

Ah, when you're torn and tattered . . .

MA NINOTTE

Give me those *dachine* things, honey. . . . I'll try to eat them after all. . . .

THE MERCHANT

They're so much . . .

MA NINOTTE

That's for the tomatoes?

THE MERCHANT

For the *dachines*, yes.

MA NINOTTE

Well, I won't be eating *dachines* either, my dear. . . .

THE MERCHANT

How much you want to pay for the *dachines*?

MA NINOTTE

I'll try to make a salad of *christofines*. Where can I find them?

THE MERCHANT

Take the *dachines*, sweetie.

MA NINOTTE

Weelll, I don't need them anymore. . . .

THE MERCHANT

Do me a favor, take the *dachines*, sugar. . . .

MA NINOTTE

What's your price, honey?

And the merchant named her a price that was so low Ma Ninotte picked up more than one *dachine*.

For the fish, it was different. You don't bargain with a fisherman. He never has enough and is overwhelmed with clients. What's more, a fisherman only sells to his friends, he has his people to whom he remains faithful *ad aeternam*. Ma Ninotte was on the list of three or four fishermen. She did them favors when school started in the fall, finding them shoes for their trail of children. Like a seasoned diplomat, she knew how to offer them pieces of nylon received from a Syrian who owed her for other services. As a result she had all the fish she wanted. The fishermen, knowing her tastes, put some aside for her as soon as her massive silhouette appeared behind the mob assaulting their skiff.

The fisherman returned from the reaches of Miquelon at eleven o'clock. They sailed up the Levassor Canal and anchored at the fish market. The regulars, the resellers, were all over them, dense as flies on syrup. Ma Ninotte strolled in calmly and signaled to the fisherman under siege: Hey, there, Mr. So-and-so, I'm glad to see you. . . . The fisherman barely answered her but, with a natural gesture, grabbed a half gourd and gave her as much as possible: usually redfish, the obligatory *coulirous* whitefish, two or three strombs if you please, little tunas, in the name of God, and a small taste of each blessing of the day. Over the heads of the rioting revelers, he handed it all to Ma Ninotte, who opened her basket. She didn't pay on the spot. The fisherman stopped by during the week and calculated her bill during punch hour. She paid up in cash, but also in cloths and other treasures from the Syrians.

Of the ten or twelve pounds of fish brought back every day, Ma Ninotte kept just enough for herself. She sold the rest to her friends, her merchant ladies, and her Syrians. She was greeted on our street like the Madonna. The circle was thereby closed. Ma Ninotte did well for herself. The only problem was that every day was a fish day, and every night was a fried-fish night. The flesh of a chicken appeared only on Sunday, that of a cow only once a month, and only if times were good at that. Today, the man who's paid his dues can barely stand the products of the sea on his plate. This makes the Prime Confidante ill: fish for her is a marvel of which no mouth may, or should, grow tired. "Eat fish, my son!"

At about one o'clock, her fishermen passed by for punch, gossip, or some sewing work. And they brought her what they could never sell: boxfish, lobsters, langoustines, black sharks, fighting fish, fat crabs—all oddities neglected by the city folk but that Ma Ninotte happily accommodated. The fishermen also offered her lambis pearls, a wonder worthy of the sign of the cross. She made earrings of them, or pins. The jewelers who executed her desires lost sleep over them. The lambis pearl is pink like a setting sun, irregular and satiny. It always seems pensive. It is said that Mama Dlo wears them in her hair, and the islands wore them to their tomb. Ma Ninotte held her surplus tight in tufts of cotton. She took them out for unbelievers, when Papa, holding forth on the sea in the company of his guzzlers, surprised everyone by suddenly declaring: "But did you know that the lambis possesses a pearly teardrop of great rarity? Ninotte, dear Gros-Kato, bring us the real thing." And the sight of these pearls sent them into a state of melancholy thirst.

> *Scrape the flesh in the mouth*
> *until the frozen tooth*
> *and with the bald seed*
> *experience the infinity of the circle*
> *Oh the season of* quénettes *was lived*
> *like a game*

Going out alone was for errands. The catastrophe of not enough oil. The salt that gets used up without warning. A passing friend, to honor with the sweetness of a soda or Didier water. The little boy had to go to the bar, then to the grocery store, then to the self-service market. Ma Ninotte had a credit booklet in each of these places. They noted her purchases, and she was supposed to pay at the end of the month. In reality she paid a few pennies when she had them, settled up when possible, or sang the merits of patience when the booklet scaled vertiginous heights. The booklet, in fact, was one of the serious conversations she had at night with Papa, in whispers.

At the bar he never dawdled. The proprietress didn't put up with the presence of children in this rum drinkers' den. They said such terrible things! The little boy imagined them seated in the semidarkness, weaving unspeakable conversations in Creole and French, cursing the waitress who surveyed the levels of their punch. The little boy asked for his bottle of Didier, his piece of ice, and left with a look of obedience, but with every antenna extended.

The grocery store, on the other hand, was a place to park. He roamed around for as long as possible. An old lady haunted the caged-in counter surrounded by shelves. There reigned a smell that included every smell, including the lingering odors of the cod that had been delivered or the smoked meat that had just been served. Everything was sold in crumbs. Mama said to send her two sausage slices. Mama said to weigh her out a spoonful of flour. Mama said to give her a quarter pound of beans, and three spoonfuls of rice, and a *musse* of rum, and a *roquille* of kerosene. When the list was too long, Ma Ninotte provided a scribbled paper. He was incapable of deciphering it and this made him anxious, because the proprietress, who wasn't very rich in eye vitamins, often bent over and squeaked at him, "What'd she write there, is it rum or kerosene?" He answered with whatever came into his head, so as not to seem as illiterate as he really was.

Tips of coral trees
snagging heads
detect the weakness
learn to hook the other without decapitating oneself
precise battle of flowers
the only one to name the beautiful season of a tree
its sensory accomplice

The Creole grocery store was a world unto itself. A capharnaum probably influenced by the customs of Chinese immigrants. As soon as the latter had fled the white men's sugar cane fields, they'd opened shops all around the country, selling any which way, any weight, and any size. In these times of empty pockets, it was a brilliant idea. The small shops of Fort-de-France followed the same principle. On the upper shelves sat the curiosities ordered on rare occasions: Noilly Prat, vermouth, whisky. Then came the wine shelves. They contained long bottles of very ordinary wines, covered with a dust from the old days and seemingly of interest to no one. Underneath were the tin cans (sardines, sausages, lentils, stews, salted butter, red-tinted margarine). The big tubs of lard sold by weight from wooden ladles completed the wall. Around the counter, sitting on the floor, were the sacks (of rice, dried beans, French flour) and the barrels (salted meat, oil, kerosene, rum), to which a pump was usually attached. On the ceiling hung the fly killers, sausages, clusters of garlic, and dried herbs. On the counter itself was the paper, the scale, the chocolate morsels, the bits of soap, the weights, the liquid measures, the bowls of French onions, the piles of bread—stale on one side, fresh on the other—the bunches of local onions, the jars of dried spices. Since there wasn't enough room, everything was piled on top of everything else to a point that defies description.

The little boy parks there for as long as possible, lets other customers pass in front of him, observes the rituals of this part of town. At the counter behind her grating, directly below an electric light bulb that washes out her complexion, the shopkeeper looks like an epiphytic fern. She is slow, limp in greeting, speaks with few words. Her eye comes to life only at the moment of the delicate passage of the weights on the scale: "Is that enough, Mrs. So-and-so?" The clients buy only what they've come for. Unlike the Syrians, the shopkeeper allows her few new items to be discovered; she suggests nothing, points to nothing. Her sole credo is: "What do you want? And if you don't know, come back and see me when you do."

The word on her was this: She had been married, without knowing it, to a *quimboiseur*, the kind of man loaded with money that came not from sweat-work but from commerce with the things of the night. They lived on the heights of Balata in a house with seven bathrooms, twenty-two windows, and a lightning rod. One day—that is to say, one special night—she awoke to find he wasn't by her side. She looked for him under the bed. She looked for him in the basement. She looked for him in the kitchen. She looked for him in the living room. She looked for him under the mahogany furniture, which shone like setting suns, and in each of the guest rooms, full of flowers open to the shadow. She looked for him in the attic and in the garden filled with orchids fed by the wind of thirteen days. She found him only before dawn, in what served as his office, or rather she found what he had left: a kind of thick canvas sack, limp and warm, which shivered all by itself, shining like the eye of a drowned man: his skin, yes.

The word on her continued as follows: By misfortune, out of lack of imagination probably, she did not make the connection between this horror and her husband. She grabbed it, screaming bloody murder, brought it into the garden, and, thinking she had caught a *quimbois* sent to her house, set it on fire. The thing burned for six months, producing a smell of tortoise shell and camphorated oil. Her husband reappeared six days later and, naturally, sought his skin in vain. Awakened at night, she saw him dancing in desperation by the endless fire. She recognized him not by his looks (he resembled nothing that could be recognized) but by intuition, the vapor of a loving soul that whispered to her: "Yes, it's him."

Without thinking (for it's rare that one thinks in such situations, the word on her ends), she ran into the garden and threw herself into his arms, threw herself into the arms of a suffering mass that smelled like hell's spice and cursed her thirteen times. She had to be reconstructed at Colson Hospital: a new memory put in, along with fifteen recollections to be developed, two emotions so her heart could beat, and other sorts of tastes. In addition, she was ordered to take a little pink pill for the rest of her life, which she ingurgitated every Saturday with the milk of a kid. She landed in Fort-de-France and opened her shop thanks to a remnant of money found in a drawer, just before the house began creaking, rising above the earth, and raining stones upon itself, with white dogs meandering in the hallways and pensive toads on the curtains, not to mention the fetid sticky stuff that seeped from the walls around the crucifixes. That's probably why she had trouble selling it and why the house still sits all alone, without trees or birds, without spiders or ants, rich with its furniture that doesn't rot and that no thief ever covets.

Today, the shopkeeper seems to have forgotten everything, except perhaps her pink pills and the sadness that comes over her when a fisherman burns a tortoise shell near the market. That's what they say, but better not to repeat it: people are a little mean and could add details, the mention of which might not receive grace at confession.

Sometimes the shopkeeper motioned to the little boy: "Tell your mama I need to see her," a way of saying that the booklet had gotten heavy. But she never refused to serve him, even when she said in a spicy voice, "Well, well, you'd think your mama had gone to France these days, I don't even see her in the mist of the horizon." To which the little boy responded, on Ma Ninotte's instructions:

"Mama's going to come bring you something. . . ."

"Ask her in what century, and if it will be during the *année-cannelle*."

Année-cannelle means: "never," explained Ma Ninotte, more worried than a mandarin orange held over into the February dryness. . . .

The hardest was returning merchandise. "Go tell the lady that this isn't a *roquille*. Ay-ay, that's not what I wanted, there's too much, there's not enough, it's not fresh, look, there's rat caca in it . . ." The little boy carried off the incriminated merchandise. His befuddled brain sought a diplomatic way to explain his reappearance to the grocer, especially as there was always a credit booklet in the background that was more or less at capacity. He resolved the difficulty of the approach with the generic expression: "Mama said there's a problem." The shopkeeper didn't react much. Leaning toward her grating, she simply asked, "Yeah, what kind of problem?" He then entered into the details of Ma Ninotte's protest. It could turn out like this:

"She said there's something in the lentils?"

"What kind of something, huh?"

"I didn't understand."

"What do you mean you didn't understand? There are lentils in my lentils, aren't there?

"That's right, that's what's strange."

"What's strange?"

"There are lentils plus a lentil that's not a lentil."

"You mean there's something in my lentils?"

"No, I didn't say that."

"What did you say?"

"What Mama said . . ."

"Let me see."

She herself discovered the rat caca, the dead cockroach, the abundance of little pebbles, grumbled a curse, crossed herself twice, and exchanged her wretched product without arguing.

Another possibility:

"Mama said there's a problem."

"What kind?"

"I don't know."

"Well, go back and ask her."

"She already told me."

"What'd she tell you?"

"A problem like something isn't something."

"Don't you think you should wash out your ears?"

"Oh, yeah! . . . You gave me kerosene?"

"You asked me for kerosene."

"That's funny, because Mama said she never asked anyone for kerosene."

"What about you, what did you ask me for?"

"I don't know."

"You don't know? Are you trying to be funny with me?"

"I asked for a *roquille* . . ."

"*A roquille* of what, huh?"

"Of what Mama asked you for."

"And what did she ask for?"

"A *roquille* . . ."

"A *roquille* of what?"

"Of what she wanted."

"And what did she want?"

"You gave me kerosene, right?"

"I gave, I gave, yes, I gave you kerosene."

"Well, that's the problem."

War weary, she took the kerosene and in another bottle measured a *roquille* of rum. He went off in seventh gear, praying to God not to have to go back soon.

Sweetsop
the seed unsealed
comes and brings a little heart
from seed to seed
we eat its grated soul separated
from what broken love?

The self-service store was a different world altogether. He had to hand in Ma Ninotte's list at the cash register, where a nameless lady without a history presided. It started off pleasant: "Well, well, you're Ma Ninotte's little one, wow, do you look like her, my gosh, what do you want, my son . . ." Then it was faster, more indifferent, and most of all less merciful when the booklet put on some weight: "Go tell Ma Ninotte to come and get it herself, I need to see her." Sometimes Ma Ninotte ignored the message, other times she headed off with a determined step, in a bit of a rage. The little boy would have given anything to know what followed. He watched her return, loaded down with her groceries, calmer than if nothing had ever been said.

Little by little the boy became circumspect: "Did you already pay the booklet?" Ma Ninotte would respond by asking him in Creole if he were with the police, if he were performing an investigation. There were jobs available at customs, she'd tell him, and advise him to wait until he grew a little taller to ask questions, and to get going on her errands before she got mad. This reaction made the little boy even more worried. It meant he would have to confront a lateness in payments. Because when everything was settled, Ma Ninotte would simply answer, "Yes, my dear," and smile at her littlest one, the final filth of her bowels.

The little boy practiced skimming when Ma Ninotte gave him money for an unusual errand. Upon handing her the change, he'd keep five or ten centimes, wait for the explosion, and, if it didn't come, store the fruit of his larceny in his treasure chest. From centime to centime, he could buy himself a freeze, a candy, some bubble gum. Back at the grocery store for his own purposes, he'd make his purchase beneath the wary gaze of the shopkeeper, who was nonetheless pleased that he wasn't returning anything. Skimming is an art. You have to get as many centimes as possible from the shopkeeper. She didn't give them up easily; change was pure energy, and thus rare, in those days of bargaining. "Mama said if you have extra change . . ." The second stage consisted of dissuading Ma Ninotte from counting the metallic pile he handed her. To do so, you had to tell her a made-up story, wring out a question, or make her laugh. It usually worked. But skimming carried dangerous latent possibilities: two days later, Ma Ninotte, who had relegated her coins to the buffet, might decide to count them. After which, she would call to the little boy with menacing formality, "Tell me, my dear sir, the bread costs this much, I gave you that much, and you brought me back this much; what happened to the five centimes?" In reality she tolerated skimming as something of a reward for the little one, who galloped endlessly on errands and so often confronted credit problems. Her interrogations were intended just to show him that when it came to monkey business, there was always a better monkey. . . .

Often, after he had muttered something about the missing centimes, she'd stuff the change into his hand, telling him, "*Mi ta'w*, here's your share." When his war chest increased in this way, the little boy began to beautify it, finding ways not to spend it. He lingered by the tub, cleaning his coins, rubbing them in ash and vinegar until they shone like the eyes of a black cat. He made the other little boys of the house drool—they who were equally expert in every kind of skimming but whose treasures were not so impeccably clean.

whomp!
The animal pounces on your marbles
and disappears with
the crystal
the iron
and the ball with the glorious heart
enraged, continue your game with the rough clay ball
dark season of triangles

The little boy's group began thinking about money. There were so many sweets to work for. The older ones had developed a lucrative system. Bottles had value in those days. They began by collecting them, rounding them up from under the stairs, gathering them from the gutter. They cleaned them in group sessions. Bottles, jars, and demijohns shone in the sun like sculpted diamonds. On Saturday, when the country people invaded the streets, they exhibited their bottles in front of the door on a wooden board. The little boy, posted on the sidewalk, shouted: "Beautiful bottles! Beautiful bottles! Beautiful demijohns, Beautiful demijohns!" In no time the clients stopped and began bargaining. The little girls of the group proved expert at this and far more obstinate. Before eleven o'clock the white bottles were out of stock, and the demijohns had brought in a fortune. The treasure was divided according to laws that remained strange to the little boy; the eldest measured their share by the obscure yardstick of seniority.

At one o'clock
the radio groans with funerary notices
every heart
tells its rosary of misfortunes

and with the emotion
spells out a people

A bottle had forty-seven thousand uses. In them, life was stored in little bits, in waters of a gesture, in tender liquors, in angry spirits, in seeds of a glance, in stocks of lucky lentils. You bottled the air of a passing year and approved it on sparkling full-moon nights. You kept under cork the lightest dews and the last breath of the innocent. The bottle was a rare object, a beautiful object. There existed real bottle sellers at the market. They hauled their wares in small carts, collected them here and sold there. Sometimes they bought our stock. But that was less lucrative, for these blue-lidded men, smelling of the resin of guaiacum, never bargained.

The other means of building up treasure consisted of perusing the open canals. On Saturdays the country people dropped change on the streets. These false moves sent coins rolling into the canals, opaque with dirty water. Only the most down-and-out risked their hands: to kneel on the banks and fish out change meant exhibiting a state of need. Thus the coins remained where they had fallen. All we had to do was wait for Saturday afternoon (when the city grew quiet, just before the passage of the street sweepers) and head out as a group. A magnet at the end of a string captured seven hundred nails as well as some coins. With a stick you could stir up the dirty water to reveal a metallic shimmer. When there was no water left, the canals condensed to a blackish crust, into which everything sank. Then you had to use a simple stick and sharpen your eye to recognize the roundness of a penny, the proper curve of a coin, amid the mummified objects.

Never hold on to a full wallet. Bring it to the police. To open it is to take a risk. A whole wallet is too lucky, too easy not to be a sin.

There was a little of everything in the open canals of Fort-de-France. Valuable objects, of course, but also old, bluish *mantou* crabs. Covered with raised hairs, they lifted menacing claws in our direction. The big kids said they weren't crabs but old Negroes toppled from a deal with the zippity-devil. Perhaps having failed to honor their pact, they had seen their wealth dry up, their business unravel, and their bodies become transformed. One morning, as they were shaving, the mirror had sent them the bad news: a bit of fur here, a budding shell there. They found themselves forced to hide in the woods, then in the mangrove swamps, then in holes, then in the canals where they ran no risk of encountering real *mantous*, who weren't very friendly toward them. Jeanne-Yvette, of course, confirmed this story.

Intrigued, the little boy began observing the *mantous* as best he could, attempting to catch a glimmer of humanity in their eyes. Though terrified by these demoniacal creatures, he was ready to find a way to break the curse. He never saw anything in their eyes on stilts and was never brave enough to grab one and check whether its crabby nature preserved some sign of its prior life. You never found dead ones; they seemed to live cemented in time, their only season a relentless pain. Jeanne-Yvette explained that by dint of flinging their humanity against the prickly carapace, the little wretches withered and became part of the mud forever encrusted in the canal waters. "The shell was left empty, indestructible, filled with a long sigh," she murmured, moonstruck.

"He's the son of Ma Ninotte and one of the mailmen, they're Lamentin people, my dear, they say that . . ." The little boy was polite, strolling among the grownups. They had authority over him and were never to be affronted with a direct gaze. Anyone who complained about him to Ma Ninotte was greeted like family.

The *mantous* surfaced in those canals the street sweepers didn't clean. They struck their war poses amid antique church medals, broken rosary beads, discolored religious images, pieces of railings, and little magic remedies in plastic packets, which sent us stampeding.

The canal proceeds were used mostly for the four-o'clock-movie shows. On Sunday afternoons, the city kids converged like a line of ants toward the Pax cinema, in front of the presbytery. The little boy was dressed as if for a baptism, in his gray wool shorts, his black shoes, his white church shirt, hair parted on the side. In a breeze of cologne water, his brothers and he and the rest of the troop descended. You had to get there early, for the battle was fierce. Cling to the gates, wait for the rush. No patient, orderly, respectful line, but an assault without quarter or mercy surrounded the booth where a cool *chabin* sold tickets first come first served. The little boy didn't have to fight; Paul or one of the big kids took care of it. From a protected corner, in the company of the youngsters, he watched the frightful, seething mass. The wait was sometimes cruel. Paul could emerge from the ticket counter only to report that the seats were sold out. And no more seats meant that the slightest space, with or without a seat, was packed with a mountain of spectators.

Once he reached the counter, the movie-going combatant dug in his heels, and his friends, brothers, cousins, schoolmates, and distant acquaintances passed him their money and ordered numerous tickets. Thus each combatant extracted from the counter no less than a dozen seats. This communal practice sometimes degenerated into a system of pillage. As a result it was possible to be two inches from victory and get crucified behind an arrival who shamelessly depleted the remaining places, while his generals, three yards to the rear, cynically organized the sacking.

Leaving 97

Not getting a seat was a terrible blow, for which no remedy existed. There was nothing else to do at that point but listlessly chew two packets of pistachios under the tamarind trees of the Savannah. The Savannah was the square where everyone strolled. From a kiosk a municipal orchestra blared civilized music. Talk at the old people's bench reordered the world around girlish crushes, the flow of young babbling. Beneath the coolness of low-hanging branches, sweets merchants offered sins for the mouth. Strolling up and down, arm in another arm far hotter than one's own, you shook off the sluggishness of a siesta and the asphyxiation of troubling thoughts. It wasn't a place for children. The little boy, locked out of the movie house, found himself doing penance there. Only later would he appreciate it, at the moment, alas, when the Savannah would lose a part of its soul beneath the aging trees, along alleys sheltering only an abulic echo of their former sighs, drowned in the empty kiosk.

But most often, the fighting big kid emerged from the riot with a clenched fist. He opened it to reveal a crush of little pink cardboard pieces, sending us into a state of unmitigated joy. In our madness, we began cursing the ticket plunderers to show them our love of life. And we'd storm the temple of the image, sitting on the floor or on wooden chairs, in an ambiance reminiscent of drunken village fairs. The joy of being there sent a merry frenzy gushing from us all. We couldn't sit still, we had to keep getting up, hailing our great deeds, signaling our presence to attest to our victory. With a circular glance, we took the occasion to note the invisible enemies of the week; erect in the seats we couldn't abandon, we threatened them from afar, sending our voices roaring over the roar. In fact, the spectacle had already begun. The comics performed before this windfall of an audience. The talkers and jokers stood straight in a jovial circus we encouraged. At the time there was no such thing as applause, but there were precise modulations of the throat, which the Creole language of today has lost.

Sometimes a Major arrived tardy and couldn't find a seat. Majors were a category of permanent warriors, men of combat, dominators, who reigned over a neighborhood, a street, a part of the world, and divided up the city into innumerable fiefdoms. For them not to sit in a proper seat during a movie was unthinkable. The delayed Major entered, braying, *"Mi mwen,"* Here I am. This arrival provoked a viscous silence, for everyone was at risk of losing his seat, except, of course, the other Majors who were already seated. A Major never attacked another Major, except for matters of territory or protection. Thus the tardy Major advanced amid a ghostly silence, his caterpillar ugliness accentuated by his unholy manners. The rows he passed began breathing again, the ones he approached with his abominable eyes suffocated on the spot. The Majors sat in the first three rows, whose seats were the most desirable: it was like sitting inside the screen. When he reached the front, the late Major marched into the already full row and flopped into the seat he had chosen, on top of the knees of a terrified victim.

What followed could take several turns. The little boy witnessed every scenario over the course of his young Sundays. *First the simplest:* the unlucky one gets up and goes to sit in a corner of free floor space, mumbling: "Excuse me, boss, I didn't know it was your seat." *The most tragic:* the unlucky victim bristles. The Major, who asks for nothing better, brings him down. First he breaks his spirit with two or three words, something about his mother, then he cuffs him, ordering him to go lie down like a hairless dog. Those around them separate into a cautious circle and return to their places only when the Major is reseated. *The bloodiest and also the rarest:* the unlucky moviegoer fights. He pulls out his pocket knife without even getting a chance to raise it, for the Major has already signed his name six or seven times with his furrowing razor. A commotion ensues; everyone heads for the doors. The movie show then starts late, after the arrival of the police and the disappearance of the combatants.

Sometimes the late Major chose the seat of another Major's protégé. This unfortunate individual remained seated beneath the aggressor, waiting for his protector to assert himself. This didn't take long. The protector, who was already seated, rose from somewhere and called to the other with the slowness of a Western film:

"Say, Mr. Something-or-other, didn't you notice you were sitting on someone? And that that someone is my little brother, the blood of my blood and the flesh of my own mama, who passed on without communion?"

"I hear a dog barking but I don't see anyone. What dog means to speak but only barks?"

"Dogs don't speak, excepting perhaps yourself."

Then came (before the conflict, which would have been awful) the identification. It could occur in words ("Ask for me, Charlot-zouti, at the thirteenth fountain of the canal . . ."), but most often it was silent. They recognized one another, evaluated one another, counted the scars (or the surface of the skin that had managed to remain healthy), and the second Major changed seats. He collapsed onto someone else nearby, who ran to the devil as fast as he could, without counting his change.

For the film to begin, two rows of windows situated at the top of the room had to be darkened. They were accessed via snakelike footbridges. The man who performed this delectable operation was a certain Tintin (so named thanks to a hairdo that came to a point above his forehead). He was beckoned with loud cries when he was late, and his appearance, which signaled the imminence of the film, received an ovation. Thus every Sunday, year after year, Tintin had his minutes of glory. He closed the windows one by one. Each closure was hailed as a Herculean feat.

The room slowly lost its light. The darkness caught our breath, thus instilling a relative silence. We settled comfortably into our seats, we spread our toes, we unraveled our packets of pistachios. A newfound innocence rounded the eyelids, slackened the jaws beneath gaping mouths. Those most nervous whistled a loud shuuuttt, getting irritated at their own sound. Tintin disappeared behind the screen. You could hear him turning the crank of the curtain, which resisted, got stuck, closed up, exhausted us to the hilt, then, suddenly liberated, opened onto the magic whiteness of the screen on which the Gaumont newsreels instantly appeared.

The films were tales of swords, great Roman spectacles, Westerns, detective stories. It was Hercules, Maciste, Robin Hood, Tarzan, Django. The traitors could be spotted by their black beards, their shifty close-up gazes and their Mediterranean tints. In the Westerns, the Indians deserved every massacre. The Chinese laundrymen repeated mechanical servilities with a nasal twang. The blacks were half idiots, with big roving eyes, constantly in terror. They filled the landscape with zealous domestics, blissful bartenders, jazz statues, savages endlessly gesturing and jagged. Their appearance elicited widespread laughter from the audience, which grew nervous. The little black boy perceived no commonality between himself and this representation. Indigenous meant black, wild, and often mean. We were Tarzan and never the half monkeys he defeated. The mechanisms of film functioned full steam. We identified with the strongest, who were always white, often blond, with eyes of celestial innocence, forcing us into internal ruin without our realizing it. It would take a major revolution for the little boy to subsequently consider himself black and obstinately learn to be so. Later, he had to learn to be Creole.

The moving picture is a dream! We lost our footing on the screen. We leapt to the emotions of the music. We absorbed the feelings and the tenderness. This meant sweating in the fights, shivering in the snow, becoming breathless during chase scenes, sliding under our seats when the close-up of a Colt murderously targeted the theater. We died a theatrical death when a Good Guy was hit. The traitors were threatened out loud, the weak women, who weighed down the action, disdainfully dismissed to their lowly status. There reigned a racket with no mama to witness. The only thing that could bring quiet was a mounting of suspense, a freezing of anxiety brought on by a throbbing note sustained in crescendo. For the lead character, the hero of the film, to stupidly lose his life after a noble speech was never profitable for the director of the theater. He himself would lose a few seats as a result of the obscure responsibility to which we held him.

There was never a bad film, everything was good, everything was grand, everything was worth discussing, retelling, replaying, and miming throughout the week, to the point of exasperating Ma Ninotte, who never set foot in the cinema.

The movie hours allowed Ma Ninotte to take a break from us. She rested her spirit and her voice. We would find her placid at her sewing machine or in the middle of a sowing of multicolored scraps, fallen from her work with paper flowers. She barely questioned us about our movie, but checked that each shirt still had its buttons. The little boy launched into profound explanations about what he'd seen. Paul and Jojo always seemed to have viewed a different film. In dismay, they would ask Ma Ninotte if this delirious pipsqueak was really their little brother.

Our arrival sent the warrior back to the front. She left her sewing machine to yoke herself to the kitchen. The evening soup. The five o'clock snack bread. Preparing the laundry for the school week. The little boy had to undress, fold his clothes, and hang them in the closet. Then there was nothing left to do but kneel at the window and try to understand, as he gazed at the dead city, what exactly had escaped him in the film he had seen.

Custard-apple
all voracity sickens
in its white abundance
this season is pleasure
only at the breast of a new milk

On Sunday afternoons Fort-de-France turned silent. All that passed was a sea wind, evidenced by the dust and the crumbs of life. On certain streets the vitreous air asphyxiated plants on strapless balconies. The embroidered woodwork. The gutters. The closed shutters, slats adjusted by invisible persons. It lived a tidy life. Each entrance hinted at the cool clay of an interior courtyard at the end of its dark alley, where mulatto mistresses wallowed in daydreams. Shutters filtered the diffused purr of the end of a meal or sometimes, among the rich-folk, a piano savored amid family quietude. The little boy, meandering alone after the cinema, was just beginning to get in touch with his city. He didn't know how to determine the dates of facades, nor their styles. He felt it to be both young and old—young due to a paucity of memory, old because its wood bore the age of things rebuilt. He didn't yet know about the many fires, but sensed each house to be ruminating widowlike memories.

The cathedral livened things up. The evening mass magnetized existence. Negresses in beads, wearing their years beneath black veils and gold jewelry, hobbled down the sidewalk in slow herds. Mulattresses blossomed in the alleys, supporting their Negress mothers. *Quimboiseurs* with long nails leveled a cane of power stiffly under their arms. Already, the bells vibrated the wood. A tormented red dripping from the sky bloodied the upper facades and the dusty windows. Then—whop!—shadow swallowed everything. Chomp!—like a mongoose at the neck of a chicken.

Leaving 103

It wasn't night, it wasn't day anymore, but already there rose from nowhere the sound of the evening bugs. The little boy, still at his window, went on the alert.

The street was nothing but a play of shadows and lunar lights with sometimes, here or there, the yellow point of a streetlight. The doors of the marvelous opened at these moments, turning on their silent hinges with the slowness of growing grass. The shadows filled with the humming of dried savannahs beneath a sliver of wind. The cursed *mantous* left their waters. Rats who weren't rats went off searching for spells to conquer. A she-devil's veil fluttered beneath a balcony. The sad gallop of the three-legged horse attempted to melt into the beating of a shutter. Mechanical cars emerged without drivers at street corners, taking off in reverse. Someone who'd made a pact with a spiritual power mingled with the bats, but the noise of his wing, heavy with sadness, could be detected just the same. Sometimes a zombi pretended to be a black man emerging from the cinema; he walked swiftly as one does in the rain, but couldn't get the placement of his shadow right. And nothing could hide his lidless gaze, his silhouette, curved like a cemetery candle, the impossible bamboo flower in his ear, intended for the sentimental she-devils of his unorthodox loves. The little boy had become an expert in the ruses of the marvelous. He knew how much reality relied on it for a life to hold together. But whom could he tell? And how could he sleep in such a crowded darkness? And how could he help worring when Ma Ninotte, oblivious, blew out the last lamp?

The black drivers honked from the break of dawn as they crossed the city, long honks, short honks, delicate honks, or thirty-thousand-pounders. They honked at intersections to assert their priority, greet a friend, call to a Syrian, assure someone or other of a faithful tenderness. In the language of the horn, which they spoke fluently, they cursed, cried, laughed, expressed contentment, admiration for a marvelous backside, an unspeakable happiness. They held complicated dialogues or resonant disputes. Even when they had no pretext, they honked to check the reassuring presence of their horn, to which, once they were stuck, they attributed the occult power of abolishing bottlenecks. The city at noon became a motley shriek, which Ma Ninotte cursed from her window—and a thousand hateful honks responded in concert, without stop.

There were bedbugs, not to say so would be lying. Hence there existed a killer of bedbugs, an Englishman fated to exile. He traveled bearing a string trestle, covered with flasks with strange names, smelly balls, wet insecticides, and a load of blue powders. His call was "Pipipipipinaise!"—and no one doubted that this was his life cry. He stood at the outskirts of markets, cloaked in kindness, never seemed to be in business but rather to be doing favors. He died himself upon the disappearance of the insects he battled; he disappeared with them, on one of those unmarked days of the calendar, and a thousand seasons had to pass before we noticed not that the bedbugs were gone, but that he was.

Memory, are you taking off?

The mamas cultivated pride. For their children not to eat well was unthinkable. The hatred of the empty plate is inherent to Creole culture, it prowls throughout history and reaches as far as the city shacks. Sometimes bad luck struck unannounced. This snake (the result of a grocery-store account impossible to settle) meant no more fish, sardines, or even breadfruit; all that was left was bread and eggs. When this happened, the mama shut the door on her condition. You had to eat inside and not nose around outside where the evil eye was watching. Each family surveyed the others mercilessly. To those who could afford only margarine they flaunted their real butter. Toward those who were eating just eggs they blew the smoke of a turtle fricassee. But to those who had neither margarine nor eggs nor cod they gave without letting it show that they were giving, with a thousand tricks and precautions. Those without often refused, shrouded in a vision of their lofty would-be status, accepting only if the approach had been skillful or if the children already had bellies inflated with the raging wind. The mamas cultivated pride.

Where does childhood end? What is this dilution? And why do you wander in this dust, whose scattering you cannot contain? Memory, who remembers for you? Who fixed your laws and procedures? Who keeps inventory in your thieving caves?

Trouble meant the Pincher, a black man in a gray suit and black detective hat. We didn't know where he lived—no doubt in an annex of hell—but he worked on a street at some clockmaker's shop. He came-and-went with long strides like a red-winged troupial late for a harvest, as if life had stingily granted him on this earth but a time of time-greedy time. What's more, he hated children. One of us made the mistake of shouting something stupid at him, probably comparing him to a bat. Bearing a grudge of balsa wood, his sole pleasure from then on was to surprise us on the stairs, swoop down on us like fire on a straw hut, and pinch us to death. The alert was always given too late. The pain bit into our sides. Each of us was pinched three or four times as we fled. When we were camped at the top of the stairs we were lucky, because he had to climb with zombi steps a staircase whose creaking always betrayed him, giving us time to detect the approach of this grimacing shadow. O panic! Had we kept still in his hands, it's clear he would have strangled us slowly, writhing with pleasure. This went on for many years before he stopped coming, but we lived with an eye on the door, on the lookout for this dear Pincher, who knew how to incarnate the cruelty of the world.

There is no memory but a skeleton of the spirit, sedimented like coral, with neither chart nor compass.

From his window the little boy could detect two seasons, times that were rainy and times that weren't. Most often the fixed eye of the sun seemed to govern the world. But gradually the seasons of Ma Ninotte's life revealed themselves to be far more numerous. Her rhythms followed the power of the day and of the night. Her body was plugged into the seasons of the moon. The seasons of the yam, the *couscouche*, and the avocado regulated her daily meals. The seasonal fruits transformed the markets, the city, and the days of Ma Ninotte. Whether the fishermen were hunting redfish from the rocks or capturing wandering whitefish meant two different times; whether they worked with lines, bow nets, or drawnets produced others; this buffeted Ma Ninotte's life the way tides do longhaired medusas.

The season of the redfish was a high season. Stews and fish stocks flavored the pots. Ma Ninotte had to go back and forth a lot, for the alerted street solicited a share. These favors amplified what she obtained from the Syrians. She was more sprightly, less available but more spirited, and changed the repertory of her laundry songs. The fishermen visited her often. They had a lot of money at their disposal, and as a result needed all kinds of useless things. Ma Ninotte never stopped struggling and waging battle for a second. During whitefish season, a time of spiced fish stews and fricassees, the urgencies were different. She was more tranquil and carefree, because whitefish is abundant. She was oriented toward the vegetable market, where fish, so long as it was fresh, was considered a treasure by the merchants of the muddy ravines. The latter exchanged ordinary *thazard* for exotic roots and sinful fruits. To the red and white seasons can be added the turtle season, the oyster and big crab seasons, the *titiris* and flying-fish seasons, and those of dozens of more subtle creatures that regulated our existence.

Leaving 107

These seasons mixed together, melded together, paralleled and influenced one another, infinitely multiplied the modes of life. Ma Ninotte used these seasons to mark time, to measure where she was slipping or slowing down. With them, Ma Ninotte gauged the order of the world and the possibilities for happiness. The little boy perceived their effects all the more as he didn't understand the meaning of her actions. She seemed speeded up like a character in a silent film, in which the most minute variations are recorded.

He himself, as he grew, entered the children's seasons. This structured his mind like a calendar. The season of yo-yos, of kites, the season of marbles, which the French call *billes*, the season of cockfighting, of crabs, of *pistaches-cocochattes*, the season of carnival, the dry season, the Christmas-manger season, and the inexhaustible season of every sweet fruit (mangoes to be scraped to the white of the seed, sweetsops to be picked apart bit by bit, custard-apples with their strange milk, *caimites*, which leave behind their tender glue, oh, the guava jams that enchant the tongue . . .).

> *I remember coco plums*
> *oh I remember coco plums*

Back from mass, one of the mamas sings, "Ave Maria, our sins will be taken away." She continues in a Latin whose meaning she must be the only one to understand (and that probably derives its meaning solely from the fact that she sings in what she claims to be a holy language). You see her at the calvary — "Ave ave ave Maria" — at the Holy Week processions; she is active on Good Friday, gives her children the rattle of new vespers. She travels to every brotherhood, participates in pilgrimages and public collections at the intersections of the stations of the cross. On 30 August, she is a pilgrim of Notre-Dame de la Délivrande at Morne-Rouge. The little boy was captivated by this austere black woman — refined, aristocratic, with the gray hair of a teacher who lived with saints, prayers, and the sky, who knew the domestic divinities from the rear of the church, and who derived from the Old Testament another manner of bearing the suffering of Creole misfortune. She kept her distance from the elements of humanity not illuminated by this light, didn't joke, rarely smiled, seemed unaffected by the disappearance of water, the effects of cyclones, or by ordinary troubles, the only generous spice to life down below. In her state of fervent faith, vulgar happiness was excluded, but an inner plenitude ennobled her, and never did anything take away this powerful authority.

Ma Irénée lives from the sale of fries on the city streets. She is also an expert in certain French pastries sculpted in molds. She wears a Chinese hat, shaped like a cone. It was brought to her by the father of her two girls, a sailor cook, whose daily route was the hold of a banana boat forever laid up. She sees him only on occasion, but more often than the little boy, who never saw him. Ma Irénée is small, a little round, silent; she lives by her ovens. Her apartment resounds with frying rain. When she makes pastries in the late afternoon, the little boys of the house hover around her door, "Hello, Mrs. Irénée, hello, Ma Irénée . . ." Without a word, with just a smile in her heart, she offers us treats. She has a weakness for the smallest ones: the little boy, as well as a kind of obstinate and unpredictable roundness on legs, covered with impetigo: Minous. He is the little boy's closest enemy. They hate one another without respite, promise to castrate one another. They both know that one will kill the other on a detour of life. One of Ma Irénée's daughters is a beautiful, light-skinned *chabine*, an expert at arranging dinner parties for dolls in the company of Anastasia. The little boy never leaves when she's there. She takes care of him like a son, coddles him, carries him, refuses him nothing, never seems bothered by his whims. The little boy's heart beats better when she's around.

One of us sucked his thumb to the point of making it pale and wrinkled. He wouldn't drop it for daily life in the house, but would hide it only on the outside, for school when it began, and for the world when he knew it was watching. Ma Sirène had tried everything to dissuade him. Blows. Threats. Teasing, herbal teas, and invocations. It didn't bother us but it bothered the grownups. Soon he was being tortured. Ma Sirène dipped his thumb in a little chicken caca and a lot of spice. From then on, the unfortunate fellow experienced the tortures of Tantalus. Delicate as no child ever was, he went about in a daze, like a cowboy without his horse, the forbidden thumbs on either side of his waist. Sometimes, in the throes of life's joys (the kinds of outbursts to which children are prone), he brought one of these hateful thumbs to his mouth — regretting it for a long time afterward, to the point that one day he stopped.

O my brothers, you know this house I could never describe, its noble aura, its dusty memory. From the street it looked like a slum. It represented the gray misery of wood in a Fort-de-France that was beginning to cement its eyes shut. But for us it was a vast palace with perennial resources, an endless hallway, a stairway peopled with lives like a cranny full of dusks, a courtyard, kitchens, tubs, roofs of rusted tin where we discovered the world in its secret splendor. Situated in the midst of the city, it filtered the city. It knew how to combine light and shadow, mystery and truth. Sometimes the warmth of its old sap exhaled in the Sunday silence. It still bears our scratches and graffiti, it stores our shadows in its shadows and still whispers to me sometimes (but things that are by now incomprehensible) when I go there.

O my brothers, it is dying in its dust. It is suffocating in memories. The stairway has shrunken. The hallway has become narrow, and a warehouse has reduced it by three-fourths. The courtyard too has been reduced and seems never to have held kitchens or tubs. In the little space that remains Ma Ninotte (the only one still there) cultivates a Creole jungle fed like us by the light, by the dampness, visited by fireflies and by silences set in the diminished brilliance of the city.

O my brothers, I want you to know: the house has closed its windows one by one, quietly detaching itself from the world, gradually closing around its guardianship of an era — the fragile archive of our childhood yore.

My brothers, oh, how I want you to know.

Fort-de-France, 3 October 1989.

Glossary

Câpresse. In the French Antilles, daughter of a mulatto man and a black woman.

Chabin (m.), chabine (f.). Light-skinned person.

Quimboiseur. User of magic. The word derives from the old tradition of curing known as *Quin/Tiens Bois. Quimboiseurs* dispense ancient remedies; they are professional ritual consultants. Also, pejoratively, "evildoers" (*Texaco,* trans. Rose-Myriam Réjouis and Val Vinokurov [New York: Pantheon, 1997]). Seer; fetish priest or priestess who practices a form of witchcraft related to beah and voodoo (*School Days,* trans. Linda Coverdale [Lincoln: Univ. Nebraska Press, 1997]).

Soucougnan. Creature capable of shedding its human skin at night, flying batlike, and emitting light (*Texaco*). A sorcerer who sheds his skin to work evil on his victims (*School Days*).